Acapulco

The Doctor

Edited by: Dr. Nancy De La Zerda

3-12-15

Michael,
Thank you for your support. Enjoy the Ride!

Acapulco

The Doctor

Alfred De La Zerda

Alfred De La Zerda
The Doctor
To your health!

"Love is in the Air"

Preface

ACAPULCO

This novel is about a young naive kid who is a complete dreamer and has grown up totally sheltered under his father's wing. He has a few good friends, but is not very worldly and has always stayed close to home and really hasn't been far from the nest.

He has a lot going for himself, and knows how to handle the opposite sex. His most valuable asset is the gift of gab. He carries himself well and is very confident. He's quite the lady's man and in his time has been very successful with the ladies. Having grown up with four sisters must have given him some insight as to what women like. He uses these secrets and knowledge to manipulate the ladies.

The story has a message for our kids and anyone that is too trusting. People aren't always who they pretend to be. Things aren't always as they appear. There is no such thing as a free ride. Everything usually has consequences. Well anyway, the kid gets caught up with some strange people and goes on a trip with two total strangers, to a faraway beach in Acapulco Mexico. He has the adventure of a lifetime but encounters a few twists and turns along the way, not to mention some scary parts.

It's a racy, whirlwind adventure through the mountains of Mexico all the while he's fantasizing about getting the girl. It's funny, sexy, exciting, fast-paced and very spontaneous. A lot of sex, drugs, and rock and roll, oh and some mild violence. Most of the story takes place in and around the Holiday Inn Acapulco.

Love is definitely in the air in Acapulco and this kid encounters a lot without, hardly trying.

This story is based on a true story.

It takes place in December 1970-January 1971.

Christmas break from college can be educational too.

Chapter One

Making New Friends

It has been many years, but when I think back, it seems like only yesterday. I had just completed my first semester at San Antonio College and was on Christmas break. Still living in my parents' home, on Mistletoe Avenue where we had lived since 1957. December 22, 1970, starts out like any one of my typical days off from school. I walked into the neighborhood pool hall and grabbed a pool cue and a beer. I was by myself, just practicing, trying to improve my skills. It was about noon, and since I hadn't been challenged to a game and had no action, my thoughts turned to lunch. I paid for my time on the table and headed for a bar stool at the bar and figured I'd have one more beer before having lunch. I noticed some action on one of the 4' by 9' tables. This is where the better players play for large amounts of money. These guys are considered A players. I was pretty good and had been playing since the age of 9, but at my best, was only a B player. Nonetheless, anyone could always bet on the side, while enjoying the game and a beer. While collecting a bet from the guy next to me, I heard someone from behind me ask if I would like another bet. Not knowing who he was, I was reluctant to bet, but figured him for a sucker. After all I was betting on the winning player. We parlayed the same bet for the next three games, all of which I came out on top. Being the good sportsman, I offered to buy the guy a drink. I introduced myself and he said his name was Jeff Anderson and added he was here on vacation with his girlfriend. I mentioned I was born and raised in San Antonio and asked where they were from? Florida, Daytona Beach, he said. Jeff was dressed to the nine's, as he stood up to reach in his slacks front pocket, I was impressed, being a sharp dresser and a ladies man myself, I have good taste in clothing. Jeff paid me the fourth and final bet.

This is a lost cause, he said. I was again impressed with the size of the money roll he peeled a few bills off for me. It was the early seventies and everyone flaunted a money roll, a jelly roll, we used to call it. The bigger the better, if you got it, flaunt it, it served to entice the women and of course other gamblers. Jeff had not been affected in the least at losing four bets to me. Somehow the conversation changed to food, and I mentioned the sandwich shop across the street. We finished our beers and headed over for some lunch. They've got the best Porky Pig sandwich in town here, pulled pork and Swiss cheese on a toasted oregano Italian loaf, I promised. Jeff stepped up to the counter and ordered and paid for two Porky Pig sandwiches and two beers. He seemed to enjoy the food, but seemed anxious to get back to the bar.

    As we crossed the street back to the pool hall, Jeff said he had to call his girlfriend at the hotel. He soon reappeared at the bar where I was having a beer. He challenged me to a game of pool. His pool skills were out of my league, but Jeff assured me he just needed someone to practice with, and I agreed. We played more than a few pool games, some video games, and ended up back at the bar. We finished a drink, and Jeff soon found a cash game on one of the main money tables. I went over to the corner card table and joined in on a domino style Knock Poker cash game. Hours later as I was about to exit the front door, Jeff came up behind me and we again talked as we walked out the front door. Nice to have met you I said, maybe I'll see you tomorrow. I'm on Christmas break from school, I'll be here about noon, I said. He assured me he'd be back, as he climbed behind the wheel of a brand new beautiful red convertible Oldsmobile two door sedan. I immediately noticed the Florida plates as he drove off.

The next day as I parked my car (1969 Volkswagen Beetle bug) I noticed the red convertible was already right up front. Jeff was already in a big cash event playing pool with one of the best players in the house. The surrounding galley of spectators was at full capacity and cash was being passed around after every game. Jeff had brought his A game, but was in over his head and didn't even know it. He had a very frustrated look on his face as we made eye contact. The match seemed to see-saw a bit, Jeff would win a game, lose two or three, win one, lose two or three. As everyone watched, the outcome was inevitable, very bleak. The uphill battle came to a crashing end as Jeff unscrewed his two-piece pool cue. I could tell by the look on his face, he must have lost a lot. Jeff walked up to me and asked me who that guy was. I explained, quite frankly, that he had just lost to a top player, and this particular player was very well off and never got nervous or choked. He's very wealthy, I explained. He can afford to win or lose without much pressure, which is a big advantage, seeing how most players don't have his size of bank roll. We sat down at the bar and ordered two beers, and two tequila shots. Here's to better days, I said, as we downed our tequila. Jeff called his girlfriend at the hotel, and said he'd be right back, and left.

Jeff was not known by anyone I spoke with at the pool hall, be it as it may, I was very curious about his girlfriend, and wondered what she would look and be like, for that matter. Jeff was much older than I, I'm guessing, maybe thirty three. From what I'd seen of him he was always dressed to the nine's, well groomed, clean cut and overall a very professional appearance. He appeared and had the mannerism of a very wealthy man. So of course I figured he would walk in with a foxy chick. My curiosity was killing me. I had a couple of more beers and was about to leave, when in walked Jeff. She looked like an absolute angel. Beautiful long blonde hair, just past her shoulders, she appeared to be about my age (eighteen or nineteen). She had a tantalizing smile, and was wearing a short beautiful dress and nice silk stockings. Jeff approached, and began my introduction to his girlfriend. She was amazingly young. As she got closer, I smelled some nice perfume, and was taken aback by the smooth skin on her face, oh so smooth, baby-like smoothness. Her hand was soft, as I shook it. I gasped for a breath as she leaned forward and I could see quite a bit of cleavage. This is Sandy, Jeff said. I could hardly speak and was glad she immediately said she wanted to play pool. We all grabbed a pool cue, ordered some drinks, and a pitcher of beer. As we approached the pool table, Jeff insisted we go on without him for he had to make a long distance phone call. He took quite some time, and while he was gone, Sandy appeared to be coming on to me. I was in a trance, she was just too much for me to handle. I was putty in her hand. When Jeff came back he sat down, grabbed his drink and insisted we continue to play without him. I figured he had enough pool for one day, especially since he had lost earlier. After about an hour of pool and drinking, Jeff insisted I join them for a sandwich across the street. I wasn't going anywhere and agreed, as Jeff paid for our pool session and bar tab. Kind of buzzed, we scurried out the front door.

While having our lunch, Jeff mentioned he was expecting a package to arrive via Greyhound Bus Line, the next day. Much to my surprise, he asked if I could do them a favor. Jeff asked if I knew or had a place they could stay the night for the package was to bring money and some other goodies, he promised. I would be greatly compensated for the favor and they would share some of the money and goodies with me. It all sounded like fun, and I just happened to be apartment sitting for one of my girlfriends, while she was out of town. How perfect, my first chance to impress Sandy, I thought. I didn't have nor could afford my own place. I was a full-time student at San Antonio College, lived with my parents and didn't have a job. I was an excellent gambler and made my spending money the fast and easy way, gambling. Oh there were times when I would lose and I would be down and out for days. When this happened, I would ask my dad for money and start all over again, building another jelly roll, as we called it. I figured Jeff had lost most of his money and could not afford the hotel room till he received the package he was expecting. So without thinking twice, I said I would help them out and let them stay with me at the apartment.

Chapter Two

Simply Persuaded

Sandy and Jeff followed me in the convertible. As we headed towards the apartment, my mind was on Sandy and didn't really know what to expect from either one of my new friends. The pad was not far and we arrived rather quickly. I was eager to please, and without hesitation offered them the bedroom and said I would sleep on the couch. They both smiled, as Jeff entered the bedroom and placed their bags and a suitcase on the neatly made bed. Jeff joined Sandy and I back in the living room. I offered up drinks, beer and some Mexican tequila. I put on a very romantic Bee Gee's album and the mood was set for my fascination with Sandy. She still had that look in her eyes like she really thought I was cool. As the conversation went on, drinks and a joint were passed around. Jeff mentioned they were planning on going to Mexico after picking up the package at the bus station the following day. What part of Mexico, I asked curiously? I don't care as long as we end up on the beach so I can try on my new bikini, Sandy said. Jeff interrupted and said, Acapulco, is there a better beach than that? I immediately knew this would be a long and eventful trip, for the beaches of Mexico were not close to any border I had ever been to. My imagination started to wander and I knew I really wanted to go, but didn't dare say so. I mentioned that my family on my mother's side all lived in Mexico, and that I'd been quite often. Jeff and Sandy looked at each other and immediately shared a large grin which made me hopeful of an invite, but nothing was said about me joining them. I sensed something was up between them but wasn't exactly sure what they were thinking. I'll never forget the look on Jeff's face as he must have thought to himself, (unbelievable, this kid is perfect for our much needed assistance to get across the border and into Mexico). He will serve as a translator, driver, what's not to like about this kid, Jeff thought. Sandy was also in a deep trance like state. (Thinking, I really like this Latin lover). He could be very helpful attending to Jeff's every command. As I handed Sandy a plate of bean and cheese nachos, she thought, I totally agree with Jeff, and know what I need to do next. I served up another round of drinks, we were all quite wasted. I visualized Sandy in her tiny bikini. I was very turned on by the thought of me having a chance to go on this exciting adventure. Jeff had excused himself and reappeared after going to the bathroom. I'm so tired, good night. Join me later when you're done partying, he said to Sandy. She gave him a big smile as if to say that's just what she wanted. She seemed somewhat childish in a way, but I could tell she was used to getting what she wanted from Jeff. Almost immediately she moved from the couch to the carpeted floor. She leaned back against the couch smiling as she propped her legs up with her arms, like a naive young girl knowing quite well that she was teasing and exposing her beautiful thighs and panties for me. With the door slightly opened, about an inch or two, I began to get a little paranoid/suspicious, was Jeff watching us, is this exciting him? I could tell Sandy was enjoying me drool like a puppy. Something wasn't quite right, I was thinking with the head on my shoulders but the other head was leading the way. She had a joint in one hand as she patted the carpeted floor between her legs, and motioned for me to come towards her with the other. As I reached for the joint, she pulled my hand and gave me a peck on the lips. My heart was racing as I moved in a little closer. I guess she was wondering how far I would go. Usually on the up and up concerning someone's girlfriend, I tried to play it off, knowing very well the door to the bedroom was opened and pretended to ignore her and held back from making the next move. She was really teasing me, and I was beginning to think that she wanted something from me. Sandy began talking about how she really liked me, and how badly she wanted me to go to Acapulco with them. Sandy went on to mention that she was going to convince Jeff. At that moment, just the mere thought of going made me almost climax in my pants. Just picture the position I was in, I was no slouch with the ladies, I've had my fair share, maybe even a few extra. But at that particular instance, I was very, very, close to her beautiful body and it seemed to me that's where she wanted me. There were a lot of vibes between us, I was hot and very turned on and she knew it. Without warning she quickly grabbed my hands and she put them high up on her thighs. I leaned forward, gave her a kiss on the lips and was getting a little braver every second. I figured I'd gamble on getting caught, Sandy was worth it. She mentioned Mexico again, got up off the floor, said good night, and headed for the bedroom. To say the least I was left in serious need of a cold shower.

Chapter Three

The Package

In the morning, first thing, Jeff called the Greyhound Bus Station and confirmed that indeed, the package had arrived and was in the name of Jeff Anderson, please have a picture I. D. he was informed by whomever he was speaking to. My new friends seemed to have a surge of energy, and got quite excited by the arrival of this special package. We all quickly dressed and headed downtown. We arrived in no time at all, seeing how we were only about fifteen minutes from the station. We all three went in and picked up the package. In a flash we were headed back to the apartment. Upon arriving, it was obvious Jeff didn't want me to see the entire contents of the package. He headed directly into the bedroom, placing the parcel on the bed. He was in sight from the living room couch where Sandy and I were sitting. I was content on staying put. He first pulled out a large vanilla folder envelope. We were both watching him through the slight opening of the bedroom door. Sandy was just as curious as I was to see what was next. He poured the contents of the envelope onto the bed. It appeared to be lots of cash and some sort of letter, because, he began to read it immediately. I was never certain or was it ever mentioned, but I think the package was sent to him by his parents, or maybe even by himself. Jeff entered the room and ordered Sandy to start packing, we're headed for Acapulco, he announced. They both had a grin from ear to ear. Jeff also mentioned that all the goodies were in the box, as he opened both hands palms up, holding two different kinds of pills in one hand, and a small bag of marijuana in the other. He told Sandy that all the documents were in order, birth certificates, passports, title to the car, and Jeff smiled, as he pulled out a Gold American Express card, we're all set, let's hurry.

How would you like to join us? If you want to go on a nice vacation with lots of perks, just say yes. All expenses paid, and you'll earn your keep by translating, driving, and being our tour guide. You know the language, and we don't speak a word. We've never been to Texas, much less Mexico. You've traveled the highways across the border and have family and some connections. You're a much valued commodity, please accept my offer. It was a no brainer for me, and said I would have to get permission from my parents, mostly my dad. I mentioned I had little money, only about eighty dollars. Not to worry, I've got you covered, said Jeff. Sandy smiled and said, I promise you won't regret it. Well it's up to my dad now, I thought to myself. I'm a pretty good judge of character, and figured I was fairly safe with my new friends. Besides I was so hot for Sandy and was eager to please. We cleaned up my friend's apartment, and headed down the steps to the vehicles. I need a little time to discuss this with my parents. We agreed to meet back at the pool hall, we'll give you an hour, Jeff said. If you're not back, we'll assume you're not going. The pressure was on, I didn't have much time but it was worth a shot, I figured.

While I'm at my parent's, Jeff tells Sandy that she's earned a big surprise and assures her once they're in Acapulco she'll get it. I sure hope this kid can go. We need to get across the border and into Mexico quick, Jeff thought. The events leading up to this point had been moving rather quickly and I was very hyped up with emotional anticipation. The adventurous trip, with Sandy in the back of my mind the whole time seemed a little farfetched, but not impossible. My hopes were high and I usually got what I wanted from my dad. I got to my house, it was about lunch time and my mother was making some of her usual Mexican cuisine. I rarely ever missed her meals, she was the best cook. I figured I'd take a shower and go at this permission thing one step at a time. By the time I was dressed, my dad was already at the dining room table. I don't recall if any of my sisters were around, but my dad noticed I was dressed nicely and asked where I was going? Well, that depends on you, I answered, as I took a big bite of a bean taco. Dad must have figured I needed some money, or maybe his car to impress a new girl. Well anyway, my mom sat down and one of my sisters joined us at the dinner table. Nearing the end of lunch I mentioned that some new friends had invited me along on a trip to Acapulco. Oh, here it comes, you need money. No, no quite frankly he's going to pay my expenses and give me spending money. And seeing how I'm on Christmas break, I thought it would be cool to go dad, can I please go dad, please? My dad must have been in a good mood for as long as it wasn't going to cost him anything he went along with the idea and said it might be fun being a tour guide, as we all laughed. My mom gave her blessing, and I was off to pack. I promised them I would be careful and would call when I got the chance.

It didn't take long to pack and split from the family scene, and was at the pool hall in a flash. They were still waiting for me and seemed very pleased I was able to get permission from my folks. They followed me home as to leave my car, which was only three blocks from the pool hall.

Chapter Four

The Road Trip

They pulled up behind me at the house, I put my small suitcase in the trunk, and went in to leave the car keys and say one last goodbye. I gave my mom a kiss and hugged dad, thanks again for letting me go. Be careful son, this trip sounds too good to be true, adios, vaya con Dios. Jeff wanted me to drive right away so I got behind the steering wheel, with Sandy in the middle, we headed for the highway.

We had traveled about forty five miles on I H 35 South and as I turned right to get on Hwy. 57, to Eagle Pass Texas and the Mexican border town Piedras Negras, I mentioned birth certificates, passports, and the title to the car. Jeff started looking in the glove compartment. No hurry, I said, we still have another hundred miles or so to go before we get to the border. Just be prepared and organized please. I wasn't sure what documents they had brought along, but I was quite confident about getting across because I am the master of the process. I had a lot of experience crossing the border, after so many years of riding along with my parents. I explained to them not to panic under any circumstances, remain calm, remember to keep your mouth shut, and let me do all the talking, please. Before crossing the border we fueled up, and got something to eat.

As we approached the first check point immediately as you enter the border town of Piedras Negras, (Black Rocks) in English, the Mexican agents got suspicious right away when the license plate numbers on the car didn't match the numbers on the car title. New plates, I said, I was doing all the talking in Spanish of course. They seemed ok with that and went on to ask Sandy if she was married to Jeff? I translated, and she said no. Upon examining her birth certificate, to my amazement, it turned out Sandy was only sixteen years old, according to her birth certificate. If she's not married to this man, she needs to be eighteen years old or have a letter from her parents giving her permission to cross into Mexico with you two fine gentlemen, he said with a snicker. I freaked out, got a little nervous, and was relieved when I heard one of the agents chuckle as he turned to the other agents and said, he had just discovered where their dinner money was coming from. Before I could even get a bill out of my wallet, the questioning continued, as if to say they weren't expecting a small bribe the way things were going. It was Jeff's turn and the trouble just kept on coming, for a moment there I was scared, but tried hard not to show it. They wanted a credit card and a birth certificate, or passport from Jeff, seeing how the car was in his name. Well the first name on the credit card was different from the first name on the passport, the last names match, thank goodness. It was the same ordeal with the driver's license and the car title, the first name was different. I began to conger up a magnificent story about how in the United States it was different than in Mexico. We'll switch the first name and the middle name around, and change it, or maybe not even use the first name and use the middle name. As far as initials, hell, to us they don't mean much. It's the last name that matters, isn't it sir? Sandy had this look of panic in her eyes, and asked to be excused to the nearest ladies room. Jeff accompanied her, as one of the agents pointed out the way down a narrow hallway. Finally, after weaving my way around every possible question and answering all with many excuses, I finally convinced them our intentions in Mexico were strictly for sunning on the beaches of Acapulco. After reaching for my back pocket, slowly of course, as to read the expressions on their faces, I could tell that they had been anticipating the motion to reach for the wallet and money. Now, I knew exactly what to do. Timing is everything when it comes down to the moment of precisely when to give up the bribe money. But, how much do you give them? You have to be able to read the person you're bribing, making the minimum amount possible easier. I quickly removed three twenty dollar bills from my wallet. One of the agents peered inside my wallet as to see how much I had. One of the agents motioned back and forth with his arms and made it clear to me that there were four of them, making it obvious they wanted that last twenty that the agent had seen. Making a lot of sense, twenty dollars each, I quickly gave it up. That left me with a few one dollar bills I had in my trouser pocket. Money well spent, I thought to myself, I just wanted those permits. Sandy and Jeff returned, and we were back in the convertible, permits in hand. I explained the money situation to Jeff and he said he would gladly return my money and much more, good job buddy. My conscious was telling me to be careful with my new friends. I was wondering what other kinds of secrets they must have. But I threw caution to the wind and didn't even ask for an explanation of the problems that had just transpired. I was too excited about the beaches of Acapulco to question their integrity, as I stepped on the gas pedal.

Now back on Hwy 57 South, a road I had been traveling all my life. My dad would bring my mother and all of us every summer to Monclova. All of my mother's family lived there. We would also visit for the Christmas holidays some years. It's a small town, most people worked at the steel mill, or railroad yard. My mom's father, my grandfather, was a railroad conductor. After my grandfather was killed in an accident at work on the railroad yard, my grandmother converted the living room entrance (double doors) into a small general store. Making small loans and selling just about anything you could imagine. She would give all the locals credit. She was a kind hearted woman, and worked from sun up to sun down. I knew this highway well and Monclova was about one hundred and fifty miles down the road, which in fact I had in mind for our first stop. I have a lot of family there. My cousin Armando has a convenience store, and I figured we could stay the night and party with him and his wife. It was about ten o'clock in the evening and I could see that the lights to Armando's corner store were still on so I knew he was there. As we pulled up some of his five children were playing in front of the store. I greeted them and asked for their dad. What a miracle, he said, (que milagro) what a miracle it is to see you, he repeats the very popular Mexican quote. Armando was always happy to see me, we were very close. I would remind him of his younger days in the U.S. Armando was born in Monclova but grew up in Chicago, where my uncle worked. After Vietnam, he came back to his hometown and got married. He offered us his small but comfortable house for the night. Jeff said, thanks but I really just wanted to meet you and get back on the road, the beaches are calling, you know what I mean? Sure, I wish I had some time, it all sounds great. He offered us food and drinks as we sat in his small office area. At his desk, he opened one of the desk drawers and pulled out a small bag of marijuana. The quality of the weed Armando had is fair. Just a little better than Jeff's but it wasn't the best either. This type of grass just leaves you wanting something more potent. As we got up to leave, my cousin gave me the small bag for the road. He loaded up some sodas and beer in a small ice chest and handed it to me. I grabbed a few bags of snacks, said our goodbyes, and I gave him a big hug, thanked him and we left.

It didn't take me long to hit the snacks because we hadn't stopped to eat. We all drank some Coronas and passed the snacks around as we got back on Hwy. 57. Jeff asked if there were any more check points coming up? Not to my knowledge I said, the next big town will be Monterey, about two hours or maybe one hundred and twenty miles from here. Pull over, you need a break, I'll drive for a while, Jeff insisted. I did what he asked, and pulled safely into what appeared to be the entrance to a small ranch. He opened the trunk and appeared to be lifting the spare tire to get at something underneath. You better pee now because I'm not going to stop for a long while, he warned. Sandy thought it was funny as she got behind some cactus and bushes and lifted her skirt to relieve herself, I too took a leak. Keeping one eye on

Sandy and one on Jeff, I was wondering what he was up to. Seeing Sandy in this squatted position turned me on. We had been drinking a lot more beer than Jeff. Jeff had this weird look on his face that was rather frightening. It was his way of letting me know that he was in full control, as he got in the driver's seat for the first time since we had left San Antonio. He reached under the dash and pulled out a plastic baggie containing some black mollies and some joints. It scared the hell out of me because I didn't know we were holding drugs in the car while crossing the border. If we had been caught it would have meant a lot of jail time at the International crossing. I jumped in the back seat and hesitated for a moment before taking the small black pill from his opened hand. As we all took the mollies, Jeff assured us we would be up all night and on the beach by morning. Jeff was beginning to show a different side of his personality, and it wasn't pretty. He also began to drive very fast. My nervousness soon turned to fear as he kept on going faster and faster. Sandy seemed to be enjoying the dangerous fast curves, but I was beyond scared. She reached over the seat and grabbed my crotch as she passed me another Corona beer and said, you only live once, baby, enjoy. As Jeff continued to barrel down the highway she began to give him joint after joint and would pass one back to me every once in a while. It was nerve racking when she moved over right next to him and started giving him power hits, shot gun hits we used to call them, mouth to mouth, the joint being in her mouth. Jeff finally slowed down a bit and told Sandy to give me a shot gun. She got up on her knees turned towards me and as I approached she gave me a great big hit and smooch at the same time. This continued for miles and my thoughts turned from fear to sex, as she kept on coming on strong. All of a sudden she jumped in the back seat and gave me more hits than I really wanted. I'll have to admit I was very turned on by all of this, her skirt jacked up and all. She had this crazy look in her eyes and I was beginning to wonder if I hadn't made a mistake coming with these crazies. Jeff told her she better behave or we might have to make her a sandwich (threesome). She grabbed my crotch, licked her lips and had me going again. Every time I thought things would get better, he would do something different to make me mad or scare me. After another beer, I said it was time to stop and pee. I've really got to go bad. Jeff wouldn't have any part of that, as Sandy and Jeff looked at each other and laughed. They found it amusing that they were making me angry. I couldn't believe he wouldn't stop the car, and he suggested I pee out the window or in a beer bottle. They were really stoned and thought it was funny. Well, believe it or not I tried to piss out of the window but was having a lot of trouble with the wind. As they laughed, I grabbed an empty Corona beer bottle and attempted to finish. Sandy was watching my every move, and even offered to help hold the bottle. Jeff just continued to drive and laugh, as he turned up the music and lit up another joint. As I sat there in the back seat, my pants undone with my dong in my hand and Sandy watching, Jeff was popping another Black Molly. After finally taking a leak and throwing the bottle out the window, I had a hard time zipping up my jeans. I had started to get quite aroused and had a partial erection. Let me just remind you, Sandy has been sitting next to me the whole time. She had a hungry look in her eyes and was licking her lips the whole time she was messing with my privates. As she reached for my manhood, I was a little embarrassed but as see could see I was physically excited. Well I don't know how, but they convinced me to take another Molly and smoke some more pot, what could I do. Jeff joined us for the next round of beers as he continued driving down the road. I promise I'll stop at the next gas station. We really need some fuel, and a real bathroom break. Sandy jumped back in the front seat and mentioned she was getting hungry. We all agreed, as we pulled into a 24 hour convenience store and gas stop just as we were about to run out of fuel. Maybe next time you'll stop for a break and fuel, we got lucky this time, I said. Everyone went to the restroom. We bought some tamales, a lady was selling by the gas pumps. Then we hit the road.

After a few hundred more miles it was apparent we were coming up on Mexico City. It was a beautiful sight. The mountains surrounding the city were covered with lights. It was a mind blowing spectacle. A mirage of lights, Mexico City is huge. People live high on the mountain side, there are like ten, fifteen million people. Any chance we spend the night here, I asked? No, here take another Molly, keep up and you won't need any sleep, he said. He continued right through the city. Even after scaring me to death, he was actually a good driver. Sandy yelled. Let's just get to the beaches of Acapulco, please. Jeff slowed the vehicle to a snail's pace and eased the car onto a very small shoulder in the middle of nowhere and stopped. It was pitch black, total darkness, I was wondering what he was up to. Maybe he wants me to drive, I thought. The only lighting were the stars in the clear sky. Without saying a word, or any explanation, he got out and opened the trunk. Sandy and I got out for a much needed stretch. As we talked, Jeff was rifling through some stuff and lifted the spare tire again. He gabbed what looked like two large black plastic trash bags from underneath. I was unable to see exactly what was going on, but I knew it was a total secret. I had not seen nor was aware of these bags and wondered what else I didn't know about. Next, he opened a small duffel bag and pulled out a pair of shorts and a Hawaiian shirt, stood right there and changed. Not a bad idea, I said. The further south we got, the warmer it was getting, must have been 80 or 85 degrees. Sandy went to her suitcase and I opened mine. I told Sandy she could change in the back seat and that I would change right here where Jeff did. Jeff was busy gathering some things in the front seat as we were changing. As I got in the back seat, Sandy jumped up in front. Jeff got back out and opened the trunk again. What's up, I thought. With the trunk still opened, he came back and started the motor and pushed a button, then quickly ran to the back to the opened trunk and was moving things around very quickly. Like magic the convertible top lifted from the front and started coming down in the back, Jeff hurried to adjust the top as it came down, and made sure it was folding properly in the correct manner, I assumed. Back on Hwy. 57 and going about 80 miles an hour again, I leaned my head back and starred at the galaxy of bright stars wondering how Jeff could drive so long and so many miles without asking me to drive. I remember thinking to myself, actually praying, dear God, help me, help us down this dark road and guide us safely to Acapulco. I must have dozed off for a while, because, all of a sudden I awoke to the application of heavy braking and my body sliding forward. Very startled, I looked up to see what appeared to be a fifty gallon barrel in the middle of the highway. There was fire coming out the top. He had done a great job stopping, no screeching sounds from the tires. As we slowly approached, I knew exactly what we had come upon, but never expected it. It was the Federales, Mexico's Highway State Troopers, accompanied by some soldiers. It was a scary scene. Many of the soldiers and officers were shirtless, and they were all holding rifles or machine guns. Oh my God, I prayed, please help us. We were all stoned and had been drinking. Luckily, when we had made the pit stop and changed, I had thrown out all the empty beer bottles and roaches from the ash trays. The top was down, maybe they won't smell the weed, I hoped. I was totally paranoid to the max, as one of the federales said, get out of the car. Los permisos por favor, your permits, please. Jeff reached into the glove box and quickly handed them the appropriate paperwork. I tried to break the ice by asking, in Spanish of course, (the whole conversation is in Spanish) how much further to Acapulco? They totally ignored me, and started to search the car. Two agents checked the inside, while about four more checked the trunk. I had also put on my Hawaiian shirt and presumed the innocent tourist role, along with my two very touristy looking friends. They very quickly checked the car and it appeared we might be on our way. They couldn't or didn't seem to find anything. The one agent that did all the talking finally said Acapulco is about an hour up the road, as the others starred at the open ice chest full of ice cold Corona. You guys look like you could use a few cold ones for later, I said. Judging by the look on their faces, I grabbed an empty plastic bag and gave them about six or seven Coronas. He closed the trunk and we got back in the car. It was just before sunrise and still very dark as we headed back on to Hwy. 57. I kind of still had a lump in my throat, and said how lucky we had been. I knew that if they had smelled the weed we had just been smoking they would have searched the car a lot better. Luckily for us we were in a convertible. We all took a big breath of fresh air. I swear I can smell the beach, I said. Everyone seemed very relaxed knowing we were less than an hour from Acapulco.

Upon arriving, we went for a cruise around the city. The sun had come up and it was a beautiful morning. None of us had ever been to Acapulco, what a sight. The view of the hotels along the beach looked like a picture, or as if I was watching one of Elvis's movies. We were in heaven. We're going to be just fine. For the first time in what seemed an eternity, I felt relaxed, comfortable. To my knowledge, I was the only one who had actually dozed off for a while in the car. Apparently the effects of the Black Mollies had us all still wired to the max. We drove up and down the main drag, where all the major hotels seemed to entice you to stop and stay for a while. People on the street seemed to be smiling at us. Lots of swimsuits and people carrying bags as if they were shopping at the store front shops. It seemed to me that everyone we saw had this smile of content, and that they couldn't be happier. It was as if something was in the air. You breathe this wonderful Acapulco atmosphere and it sort of turns you on. Well that and the temperature is so perfect, your skin just tingles. The sunshine was warm, not like the burning hot sun in Texas. The sun's energy was tantalizing, and left you wanting more of the same. I wasn't sure where or when we would finally stop and get out of the car, but I was ready. Sandy finally pointed to a hotel and said, that one, please. Jeff just pulled in, got out of the car, didn't say a word, and went in the front door. He came out and we parked the car in the garage. We were all checked in and Jeff handed me my own hotel key.

Chapter Five

Merry Christmas

Our room was very nice, and had two queen size beds side by side, which amused me, and I thought, um, this could be interesting. I truly thought that they would want to rest for a while, wrong again. They opened the suitcase and pulled out their swimsuits. I gasped for a breath when Sandy emerged from the bathroom. She was incredible, long blonde hair, just past her shoulders. Large, but not too large, firm breasts, slender waist, flat stomach, perfect abs. What people in California call girls, women, and ladies, with perfect physiques, hard bodies. She definitely had one. I quickly changed into my swim suit. We grabbed a few hotel towels and headed for the beach. Acapulco Bay was unbelievable. It almost seemed like a dream. As we walked barefoot in the warm sand, it occurred to me, it seemed rather weird, and had not even been mentioned, by either of my new friends. Christmas Day! It can't be I thought. I reflected back on the past days, let's see, I met Jeff on the December 22nd, that first day, at about noon. The next day, the 23rd, I met Sandy and we all stayed at the apartment. We left for Acapulco on the 24th. We traveled all day and night. Today is the 25th. Oh my God it is Christmas Day! I had never been away from my family during the holidays and felt a little strange, kind of lonely, then I saw Sandy's bikini bottom rising up, I could get used to this, I guess I'll be alright. My new friends were unaware and really didn't seem to care, what day it ever was. No dates, times or holidays had ever been mentioned by either of them. They seemed to always be caught up in the moment, all the time, day or night. They seemed rather inseparable. The whole situation was strange. Well anyway, it still was not even mentioned. Get my drift, weird. Maybe it slipped their minds, I thought. Things had been moving along almost in fast forward, and the following events let me know that things were going to continue to do so, and that I was in for the ride or my life.

As carefree as children on the beach, we laughed and talked about how the next few days were going to be so much fun. Without a worry in the world, my eyes focus on Sandy's behind, what a sight. Jeff and Sandy were walking just ahead of me. Suddenly a young man, he looked to be about 20 years old, approached Jeff. We were still right in front of our hotel, and had only been on the beach five minutes. He carried a small brown leather bag, as he opened it to reveal some beautiful pearls. He opened his palm and poured out some of the pearls. They were large black and white pearls and looked like quite a find. The young man explained how he and his brother would snorkel and dive daily to retrieve the cultured pearls. I guarantee these are the finest cultured pearls in Acapulco, he said, as he offered to sell us his wares. Jeff and Sandy seemed very interested in buying some, especially when he said they were only a dollar apiece. As we talked, we continued moving along the beach. I was translating everything as usual. I sort of followed along behind them as they inspected the pearls. It was clear they wanted to buy some of the pearls. At that point in the conversation, Jeff asks this guy if he knew where to find some Acapulco Gold? Like magic, he raised his hand and called someone that must have been observing us, and from pretty darn close. He arrived in a matter of seconds. I couldn't believe my eyes when all of sudden there were two of these guys. They were identical twins. Both men were short, muscular builds and very dark complexions, same kinky black, sort of a short curly Afro style haircut. I kid you not, you could not tell them apart in a million years. You'd think you were seeing double right down to the Hawaiian style swim suits. As his brother approached, it was obvious he wasn't alone. He was with several other young guys but they sort of hung back a little ways. As they (the brothers) talked, (all conversations except with Sandy and Jeff were always in Spanish), one motioned the way as we continued to walk further up the beach. The other brother put his arm around my shoulder as we walked. Making small talk, I thought we had an understanding. His arm still around my shoulder, he sort of used it to guide the way. The first brother led the way, Jeff and Sandy right with him, and we were bringing up the rear. It was for sure that Jeff wanted to see the Acapulco gold. Our short journey ended right behind some huge boulders on the side and back away from the main beach area. They made for good cover for the unlawful purchase that was about to take place. Suddenly I felt my heart in my throat as my gut instinct told me something was wrong. Still buzzed from the speed, I was nervous, anxious and leery. Out of the shoulder bag the second brother was carrying, came a large aluminum foil package. In it were three long and very large buds, you could tell it was the real thing, because, when the sunshine hit the marijuana buds it glowed like Fool's Gold. We all got excited about the weed and realized the quality of this stuff and how high we could get. I'd seen it before, only once in San Antonio. We were all very impressed and Jeff wanted both the pearls and the smoke. Feeling closed in and somewhat uneasy, I stepped back and out a little and could see the beach, what a sight. That's better as I took a deep breathe. Thinking this was a done deal, I was anticipating cooling off soon as I gathered my thoughts. We hadn't even been in the ocean. From a distance, I couldn't believe what Jeff asked next. He wanted more of the Acapulco gold, and believe it or not, he asked for some Cocaine, do you guys have any? The merchant with his wares, waived his magic arm and signaled for the rest of the pack that had been hanging back to approach. I couldn't believe Jeff, he was out of control, they were all smiles, but I was nervous and very impatient. The situation was getting out of control and I was getting this uncomfortable feeling again, this is not how you do business, I thought. Suddenly we were surrounded by this mob and I knew I needed space. I was relieved when I heard one of the gang members speaking some broken English with Jeff, as I backed off again towards the open beach a few feet away. I took some deep breaths and just knew I needed to get away, I wanted no part of this transaction. Keep in mind that all this was happening very fast. This new fella pulled out a plastic bag containing, small aluminum foil square's. Each square supposedly was a gram. Jeff asked the price of the Coke and made some sort of a deal with these guys for everything. I didn't hear the exact transaction. I remained several feet away, as the deal was about to go down, the exchange of goods for the money. Jeff, to my surprise, pulled out a large bank roll of money from his swimsuit. You could see by the size of the roll it was a lot of money. The hundred dollar bills were clearly visible. I could not believe my eyes, after all one would not expect to see someone wearing a bathing suit to be carrying all that money on your person. The moment of truth was going down and everyone saw the money. Jeff seemed suspicious of the eagerness of the fellow with the Coke, and holding the money in one hand, Sandy at his side, asked to taste the Coke. As the fellow opened one of the gram squares, Jeff reached out with his finger to taste the quality. Jeff made a face and all hell broke loose. They grabbed his money roll and pushed him to the sand. Sandy turned and looked at me, thank God I was a few feet away, I yelled at her to run, as I took off down the beach. Believe it or not, if I wouldn't have had that little head start the guy chasing me with a large stick would've caught me. As I ran, in my mind I knew we had been set up. As I looked over my shoulder this guy was still chasing me, I couldn't believe it. These guys were bold, this must've been part of their routine, and because it was their turf, they appeared to be very relaxed and not one bit concerned with all the tourists on the beach. There wasn't any security or police anywhere to be seen. I guess the guy tired, but I distinctly heard him say something like, I'm going to give you a break you being a Mexican. As he stopped chasing me he spoke in Spanish, and the way I heard it, what he was saying was, that since I was Spanish, he was going to give me a break. Sandy wasn't very far behind, and fortunately for us wasn't being chased. I sat down and tried to catch my breath, as I waited for her to reach me. As she ran towards me I stood up, her breasts bouncing practically fully exposed to me, my excitement grew as she hugged me very tightly and softly put her lips on my ear lobe. As I pulled her in closely and held her tight so that our embrace pressed us together at the waistline, Sandy and I pretty much had our first little moment at this point. My hands went from her shoulders down to her lower waist and I could feel her love handles. She seemed as excited as I and we shared a brief but very sensual moment. She definitely had a hard body. Sandy was scared and asked me if I could see Jeff? He was nowhere in sight. We waited a few minutes, and could see he was slowly coming our way. Jeff was really upset. He tried to blame the whole thing on me. You speak Spanish, you know the language. You knew what was going on. I hesitated to answer but didn't back down from his accusations. Me I said, I wasn't the one who wanted more, more, more. You were the one who brought up the Acapulco gold, and the cocaine. Everything was going fine, and to this day I truly believe if Jeff hadn't been so arrogant, so demanding about wanting everything he could get his hands on all at once, they probably wouldn't have thought we were such pigeons. It seems to me that you were at fault, especially when you pulled out the money roll. No one in their right mind would have ever been that stupid. What did you expect from these punks anyway, the red carpet treatment? You were clearly not thinking. I figured Jeff had stashed some of his money in the hotel room. Or maybe in the car, like I would've done. Never expecting to see that much money, the thugs took advantage, it was probably the most money they'd seen all year at one opportune time. I can't really blame them, you are so stupid. For a minute there I thought he was going to hit me, he was frantic. I backed off a little bit, and asked how much of his money they had gotten. All of it, Jeff replied. Panic set in as we headed for the parking garage basement where we had parked the convertible. Once we got to the car, Jeff jumped behind the wheel and said for us to stand still and told us not to move. Sandy and I just froze in position, as not to upset Jeff any further. We had no idea what Jeff was up to but he was moving very fast. He pushed a button on the dash board of the convertible. The top on the convertible sedan was still in the down position. It started to come up from the back slowly. When the convertible top was midway he pushed the button and it stopped. Jeff shut off the engine. Then jumped out of the car and came around to the back of the car where we were still standing. He was furious and was mumbling on and on about how we were going to get these guys right now. Underneath where the car top had been sitting was his hiding place. Just then I realized. What he had done with the two black plastic trash bags he had stashed just before we had changed clothes and hit the roadblock, and put the top down. I'm not sure if Sandy knew what was inside, but I couldn't believe what he was pulling out of the bags. Jeff had two large handguns fully loaded. They scared the hell out of me. Sandy put them in her purse and Jeff said, let's go to the beach and find these guys. I had no choice but to go along.

My stuff was in the hotel, I didn't have any money. I had stashed the thirty or so dollars in small bills he had given me in the hotel. I really didn't have any other idea on what to do at that moment. You've got to remember that everything in this story is moving along very fast, it wasn't even 10 am yet. It was December 25, 1971 Christmas day, the thugs were long gone. The beach looked as if nothing had gone down. I really don't think anyone even noticed the sting. These guys were smart, probably already celebrating, somewhere far from the scene of the crime. After about 30 min. of searching for these guys on the beach, Jeff finally agreed to go back to the hotel room.

Upon arriving I thought we would rest, maybe get something to eat, but of course I was wrong, no, Jeff had a weird way of thinking. I had never had any experience with someone whose mind worked the way Jeff's did. I was getting very nervous and scared. If only I hadn't come. I prayed. Dear Lord, please watch over me. To my surprise, Jeff ordered us to quickly get our belongings, and informed us that we were leaving the hotel. We hadn't unpacked or moved a thing in the room and it looked as if we had never even been there. We made a clean getaway and no one even questioned us on the way out of the hotel.

Chapter Six

The Stay

As we drove back to the main strip, I wondered where we were going. Sandy pointed upward to a hotel, apparently she really liked. Without saying a word Jeff just quickly pulled into the tallest hotel we had seen that day. It must have been 30 stories tall. Jeff and Sandy went in, as I sat and took care of the car out in front of the hotel. I looked toward the front doors, and could see Sandy and Jeff exiting. The large sign in front of the hotel said, Holiday Inn. They were smiling, as if they were on their honeymoon. Jeff looked at me and explained everything was going to be all right. I used my Gold American Express card and got us a room, even better than the first, he said smiling. Just like if everything that had just happened to us was long forgotten. This guy was a great con, he carried himself well, always very confident of his decisions. Low and behold he had me right where he wanted me again, trusting him. It was hard not to, I really didn't have much of a choice, as he handed me my own key to the hotel room. We parked the car in the hotel parking garage, emptied the trunk and went into the lobby. Hotel staff took everything out of our hands and put them on a rolling cart as we headed for the elevators. The basement and first two floors were shops, restaurants, hair salons, beauty shop, and a large arcade game room for kids. There were jewelry shops, clothing, shoes, and everything you could think of. The Holiday Inn obviously was a first class hotel, probably a five-star grand hotel. The valet went on in Spanish and welcomed us to our vacation paradise. You will love the room service and the view from your room, it's the best, I know it well, he said. To my surprise we stopped on the third floor and I was little disappointed, I would have liked to go to the top I thought. After entering the room pushing our cart, the valet opened the patio curtains and I changed my mind about the floor. There was a swimming pool and swim up bar right outside our door. We probably couldn't have asked for a better room, I thought. I thanked the valet and assured him he was totally right about how great our room was. Jeff promised the kid a big tip later. As we unpacked, Jeff made it clear we would be staying here for a few days if not more, he was very impressed with the service and the room. Again, there were two queen size beds side-by-side. Sandy jumped in the shower first. As Jeff and I talked he mentioned I could sign for anything in the hotel that I needed as long as I had my hotel key. He also said his Gold American Express card would take care of all our expenses, meals and of course drinks at any of the bars, they even serve drinks on the beach, so enjoy he said. Sandy came out of the bathroom with a white hotel towel wrapped around her beautiful body, her beauty was breathtaking, stunning. Jeff told her to put on a dress for we would all be going down to lunch first, then to the beach. This sounded great, the last thing I could remember eating were the tamales we had eaten on the road, we were all starving.

At some point during our meal, Jeff had made up his mind, and mentioned he wanted to go down to the police department and report our misfortune. It sounded a bit far-fetched, but I had learned not to disagree with Jeff and just kept quiet. We finished our lunch, Jeff signed the bill, upon showing the guest hotel key and we headed for the car. On the way out, in front of the hotel I asked a cab driver for directions to the local police department. I was not looking forward to this, and thought to myself that it really wouldn't do any good. I knew I would have to do all the talking and figured it would be a little embarrassing. When we arrived at police headquarters two older officers escorted us in to a tiny office with a small desk and a single chair. One sat at the desk as the other stood and stared at Sandy from top to bottom. The one seated said, digame, which means, tell me, and then asked how can I help you? Or more specifically tell me. I began my story from the beginning and mentioned the pearls. By the expression on their faces I could tell they knew more than I was telling them right away. I was quickly interrupted by the fellow sitting at the desk. Yo entiendo, I understand he said, empesaron con las perlitas, they started with the pearls, entonces la mota, then the weed, y sigueron con la coka, verda? Next it was the coke, right! Yes, I said. They sort of chuckled and explained that this was their M.O. (method of operation). We know exactly who they are, no further need to explain, come back tonight and we will help you get your money back, what's left, that is, if there is any left. They asked a few more basic police questions and finally how much money we had lost? As they motioned towards the door they told us to come back that night at about 9 PM. The officer told us he knew exactly where to find the twins and where they would most probably be celebrating with that kind of score. I assured them we would be back and exited quickly.

Back at the hotel, we quickly undressed and jumped in our beds to finally get some much-needed rest. We slept most of the afternoon. When I awoke Sandy and Jeff were still asleep. I put on one of my new swimsuits and headed out the balcony door. Poolside, I sat at the bar and ordered a margarita, top shelf, frozen, jumbo, and a Tecate cerveza (beer) with limes, chaser. I intentionally left the sliding door and curtains open hoping to wake Sandy. I was hoping she would come out and catch some rays with me by the pool, and join me for a drink without Jeff. No such luck, so I flirted with a couple of young girls sitting by our hotel room sliding doors. In and out the doors I went hoping to get their attention, or quite possibly wake Sandy. Sandy did not move she was out like a light. I couldn't really blame them for sleeping. I figured they must have taken a Tuinaul (downer, Christmas tree). I decided to go for a swim, and sort of on purpose, tried to splash the girls laid out by our door. It worked. I finally got their attention, as I dared them for pay back. They entered the pool and we played around sort of a tagging game. I didn't really get to know the girls, as their dad obviously called them to the lunch buffet. I reentered the hotel room to find Sandy and Jeff coming out of the shower, and changing into their swimsuits. Let's head for the beach, Jeff said. I'd never seen such clear blue ocean water before, it was beautiful. It was amazing. As we sat on the beach, waiters and waitresses were all over the place taking drink orders right in front of our hotel. We were in heaven, soaking up the rays. We were drinking margaritas and chasing them down with Coronas and Tecate beers. Out in front of the hotel in the bay was a floating wooden dock. We decided it was time for a swim and all swam out to the floating dock and were enjoying just laying out floating in the ocean. People were waterskiing in the bay area right in front of the hotel. I'd never seen anyone ski in the ocean. The Bay Area was calm like a lake. As the boat approached the dock with the teens that were skiing behind it, they removed their skis and jumped on the dock. We had obviously come to where you could buy tickets or just pay the driver of the boat to ski. Timing was perfect and we were asked if we would like to be next? The captain of the boat informed us that they worked for our hotel the Holiday Inn and that we could sign for the bill as long as we had our hotel key. Jeff needed no further convincing, as Sandy and I jumped into the boat. Jeff put on the skis and said he would go first. As we pulled Jeff around the bay, Sandy sat right next to me and started coming on to me again. She knew just how to make a guy feel wanted. Well anyway, Sandy was next and I followed. We all knew how to water ski, so that just made it that much more competitive and fun. We completed our time and decided to have a late lunch at the buffet. The most food I'd ever seen, seafood galore. Oh my God, what a sight. Oysters, crab legs, shrimp cocktail, crab, you name it, it was all there. I tried the salmon and crab cake. They were out of this world. I could go on eating forever. After our crustacean sensation, we headed back to our room. We were totally exhausted. It didn't take long for all three of us to fall asleep. When I awoke, I jumped in the shower and dressed for the evening. That must've been around 8 PM. I went out the sliding door and sat out by the pool. After about 10 min, I remembered we were supposed to go to meet the policeman at the station at 9 PM. Upon reentering the room, I could see that Sandy was sleeping in the buff. As I watched her for just a second, she seemed to be smiling in her sleep. She sure looked sexy. I touched Jeff on the shoulder and told him about our appointment. He got out of bed really fast and jumped in the shower without waking Sandy. I turned on the TV, and quietly watched it and Sandy at the same time. I was turned on, but felt a little uneasy because she was very exposed, so I stepped back out to the bar and pool area to have another drink. The hotel must've been at 100% capacity. There were people everywhere you looked. It was very exciting to be around all the tourists. I had never met so many people from so many different places. I took a short walk around the third-floor level and thought to myself how lucky we had been. We actually have the best room by far. It was the only suite with the sliding balcony door right by the pool and third floor bar.

We literally had the pool and bar on our front porch. When I returned to the room, I could see Jeff was done showering and Sandy was taking her turn. He smiled at me and asked if there were any interesting people at the bar? Yes, it's very busy, I said. Well let's have a drink while Sandy gets dressed, I am going to need a stiff drink or two. As we conversed, Jeff seemed very apologetic, he went on to say, he really didn't feel like going down to the police station. He had decided to forget about it. It's not worth it. I am totally embarrassed about the whole situation. He actually apologized, and went on about how he was at fault. This guy was being very sincere, and admitted how wrong he had been towards me. He then reached out his hand and offered an apologetic shake. As I shook his hand, I looked him straight in the eye, apology accepted. I took a deep breath and felt relieved. I had not been looking forward to going. He ordered another round of drinks. It was as if I was starting to realize Jeff had a Dr. Jekyll and Mr. Hyde personality. He has a very persuasive and manipulative manner of acting and speaking, obviously used to being totally in charge of all situations. I really didn't have much of a choice but to hope that things would work out or begin to get better. Jeff was and is very much in charge and he and I knew it. We finished our drinks and went back to the room. Sandy was dressed and ready to go. Let's go down to dinner, she said. Jeff agreed, and off we went towards the elevator.

After a fabulous dinner, we went into one of the clubs. Later that evening we found out there were three clubs in our hotel, and were told we should visit them all because each one had different ambience. This first club was really neat. It was Salsa music, and we took turns dancing with Sandy. I noticed a good looking group of girls, about my age and asked one of them to dance. We hit it off quite nicely and I struck up some small talk, like, where are you from? Are you staying in this hotel? Etc. After dancing three in a row with her, I invited her over to meet Jeff and Sandy. Jeff offered her a drink and she accepted. She really didn't sit down to join us as we stood and continued talking. I could tell she really wanted to continue dancing. She said she was in the club with her mother and sister, and some other girls she had met at the pool. They were all very good-looking and I couldn't really pick out the mom. She took me over and introduced me to everyone. Then she led me back out on the dance floor. After about an hour of dancing and drinking, their party was calling it a night. Jeff said he was tired, so we all left together. On the way up the elevator we said our goodbyes and I casually mentioned how much I was looking forward to seeing her again tomorrow. The elevator door opened as she turned and gave me a big hug and a peck on the cheek. You better show up for our date tomorrow, I'm kidding, Peggy said, I'm sure I'll see you at noon. She was a knock out, had a sense of humor and was super gorgeous. I had no intention of missing that date. See you at about noon, right by the buffet and bar area. I promise you won't regret spending some time on the beach with this lifeguard. Swimming lessons included, she asked? Most definitely young lady, it'll be lots of fun. Jeff, Sandy and I watched some TV, well, that's a half truth, because one of my eyes was always on Sandy. She sat with Jeff on the couch and I sat straight across from them on the loveseat. Right in front of us was a glass coffee table where we placed our wine goblets on neat little coasters. We were sharing a great bottle of French wine, Poillie Fousee I think that's how you spell it? Well anyway it's sort of fruity, tangy, dry, but not too dry, a little tart, just the way I like white wine, especially French wine. I first tried this wine when I was a waiter at the country club. Funny thing is when you really like something you can really suggestively sell whatever it is very easily and enthusiastically, people notice. The midrange price and good taste probably had a lot to do with my success selling lots of bottles. I'm really more of a beer guy, but was not about to be excluded from their extravaganza. You see, Jeff always made an event out of everything. Suddenly there was a knock on the door. I wonder who that could be, Sandy asked? I opened the door to find a room service waiter standing right outside our door. He pushed the rolling cart into our room, as I proceeded to close the door behind him. On the cart were a potpourri of appetizers and another bottle of French wine and fresh wine glasses. Cheese, crackers, sausage, shrimp cocktail, oysters, goose liver pâté, even some chocolate covered strawberries for dessert. It was awesome, all very classy with cloth napkins and small glass clear appetizer plates. I was quickly learning to enjoy Jeff's way of life at his expense. I could get use to this, I thought to myself. Meanwhile, without missing a frame, I was smiling at Sandy, sitting there in this short lovely dress. Sandy was obviously smiling right back with approval. She winked at me and sort of glanced down at my bulging crotch. As she did, I also looked at hers and noticed she wasn't wearing any panties, just panty hose. To my surprise, Jeff, was not paying any attention or didn't seem to mind the show Sandy was putting on for me. Maybe he knows and is getting turned on by the situation, to this day I still don't know but I was having the time of my young life. I think Sandy was anticipating her first encounter with a Mexican American Latin lover, me. I could see it in her eyes. I think she wanted me as bad as I wanted her. The curtains were drawn, maybe the thought of someone outside watching turned them both on. Her lips seemed to glisten in the moonlight, both sets of lips. This went on till we finished the bottle of wine and most of the appetizers. Jeff decided to go to bed as Sandy pulled out a deck of cards and challenged me to a game of gin rummy. I really want to play strip poker Sandy teased. Jeff watched television from the bed, but seemed to be watching us also. The table had a glass, very clear top, which made viewing her crystal clear. Sandy shuffled the cards and dealt like a pro. We moved in closer and closer as we played cards and things started to heat up between Sandy and me. It appeared Jeff had fallen asleep. Sandy took off her high heel stilettos and put her pantyhose covered foot on my crotch underneath the table. From where Jeff lay, I don't think he could see, awake or not. At this point I really didn't care one way or the other. Suddenly, Sandy made a B-line for the bathroom. My heart was panting with desire, and I was pretty much sexually at the point of no return. I have to have Sandy right now, I thought. When Sandy returned, she sat back down and had this look of desire in her facial expression. She smiled and glanced down at my crotch again and I returned the look at her crotch. I was floored by the free and clear exposure of her vagina for the very first time. You see, she had removed her pantyhose. It's time to make my boldest move, I thought, time to risk it all. Removing my sandal, I placed my bare right foot in her crotch area as my toes went in for the kill. She was moist and felt very warm. She smiled with approval. After a couple of foot maneuvers and procedures, she shuddered with glee and reached down and removed my soaked foot, went to the bathroom to finish what I had started, I guess. She left the door slightly open as she sat on the toilet and did her thing, I moved over closer to the cracked bathroom door. I locked the door behind me. I pretended to wash my hands. I positioned myself behind the door so I could watch her without her seeing me. I decided to do my thing right along with her, seeing how it was obvious she wanted to wait. She moaned and groaned, climaxed, and jumped into the shower. After a quick rinse she dried off and went to bed. It was now my turn to shower and head for the sack.

Sandy awoke very chipper and immediately let me know with that certain childish but very cute and sexy smile, that she approved and happily accepted the pre-dawn fantasy, we both seemed to be setting up for a grand finale. It was only a matter of time before we would have our fantasy come true, the right time, the right place was so important, patience on my part was running thin.

I actually enjoy the semi-teasing, and the enjoyable fear factor but enough is enough, a man needs to know where he stands with a beautiful girl. It was time for the takedown, conquer, and the kill. The anticipation was getting to me and I was becoming very desperate to have my way with Sandy.

I never slept better, and awoke with a huge appetite, not to mention a huge erection. It was unanimous and we headed down to the breakfast buffet. After breakfast, Jeff wanted to go for a cruise in the convertible. As we passed a few shops, Sandy wanted a beautiful white bikini that was on display on a mannequin in one of the storefront windows. Please, Sandy said, I have to have that bikini. Jeff pulled into the parking lot and as we got out of the car offered to buy everyone a new swimsuit. Maybe even two, he said. Sandy tried on the white itsy bitsy bikini and looked incredible. I immediately imagined how transparent it would be once it got wet. Wow, oh wow!! Jeff must have been in a spending mood, because he offered to buy us some Hawaiian matching shirts, the kind with palm trees, flowers and button style. Then decided we all needed a few Acapulco T-shirts. Jeff and I both picked out similar matching swimsuits and Hawaiian shirts. I guess the Hawaiian look was in. When in Rome dress like the Romans, he's happy, likes the clothes obviously and he's reaching for the wallet, the Gold American Express card, fine, why not, I thought. The sales girl asked where we were from and I said, Texas. I was impressed with Jeff's generosity. Money seemed to be of no object to Jeff. We were going all out first class all the way, and it appeared that was the norm for Jeff and Sandy. We hopped back in the convertible and headed back to the hotel.

Once we were back in the suite, Jeff asked Sandy to roll some joints and we started to party. He reached under the bed and pulled out the duffel bag. Inside were the two black plastic trash bags. He reached inside one of the bags and grabbed more black mollies, along with some other red and green pills. I like to smoke pot, but wasn't into pills. Jeff mentioned the black ones are uppers and when you want to come down you take a red and green pill. The red and green pills are downers, Jeff explained. I passed on the pills, but smoked plenty of pot. Jeff mentioned that the quality of the marijuana he was sent in his package wasn't that great, and neither was the smoke my cousin, Armando gave us. That's why I wanted the

Acapulco Gold. As we sat around the room, watching TV, drinking Coronas and partying, I thought about San Antonio, and my family. I'd only been away a couple of days, (it seemed much longer). I really missed my family. After Sandy came out of the bathroom in her new white bikini, my thoughts quickly changed. She looked incredible, and Jeff spanked her on her bottom, playfully smiling with approval. We put the weed away, and Jeff opened the curtains and sliding door. It was almost noon and the tourists were all around the pool and the bar right outside our door, it was really neat. It was as if they were on our front porch. They were practically in our room they were so close. I hoped no one could smell the pot, and sprayed some of my Right Guard deodorant near the sliding door entrance. I quickly put on one of my new swimsuits and went out by the pool. It didn't take long for Jeff and Sandy to come out and join me. We were being waited on hand and foot, cocktail waitresses and waiters everywhere, Jeff ordered a round of drinks. This is the life, I thought to myself. I went into the pool for a dip and Sandy followed me in. She was very playful in the water, and I could tell she wanted some attention. Jeff jumped in and we started horse playing around with Sandy. She rode him like a horse. Next, she jumped on my back. She was definitely getting the attention she was demanding. Everyone was watching us, with a smile of approval. Being as young and beautiful as she was, all the guys and even some of the girls were watching her every move. After sitting around the pool for about another hour, we decided it was time to hit the beach. Oh by the way, the white bikini was not transparent at all. I guess she was too blonde!! We locked the sliding door, and headed out towards the elevators via the front door. The beach was crowded, but we were fortunate to find a vacant umbrella. Each hotel has the area in front of it set up with umbrellas for its guests to use. They're really not umbrellas, more like small palapas, made of large palm tree branches. In the back of my mind I was still thinking about the girl I had met at the club, Peggy, but unfortunately I hadn't seen her as of yet. Jeff and Sandy headed into the water, while I just relaxed under the shade. It was really hot, and it wasn't long before I joined them in the water. Sandy started trying to pull my swimsuit down almost as soon as I reached them. Jeff thought it was funny, I really wasn't sure just how to take it. He assured me everything was all right and told me to relax and enjoy. After a lot of horsing around and rough play, Jeff headed for the palapa. Sandy jumped on my back and rode me like a horse. She started biting my ear, and told me she had been thinking about me the night before. I was very impressed and soon put my hands on her beautiful waist and held her up high in front of me. As I looked into her eyes, she seemed to really mean it. We were face to face and she kissed me on the lips. I held her close as we embraced. It didn't take long for me to snap out of it. Just the thought of upsetting Jeff was very frightening. I told her to behave and not to get me in any trouble. We got out of the water and found Jeff ordering more drinks under the palapa. He laughed and asked me if I had a bulge in my swimsuit? I was somewhat embarrassed, but played it off when we all laughed and the subject was dropped. Leaving the beach and on the way up the steps to the main pool area there was a rinse shower. We took turns rinsing off the sand from our bodies and headed towards the main pool area and bar. At the top of the stairs was a sun deck, looking over the bay. Just behind that was the main pool and bar. Further over to the right was the buffet. We soaked up some rays on the deck, swam in the pool and then went over to the buffet and helped ourselves to endless trays of fruits and vegetables, cheese and cold cuts. After lunch, Jeff and Sandy went to the room for a nap. I stayed behind and went back over to the sundeck. I noticed a good-looking older woman that I remembered reading a book right outside our room earlier that morning and quickly took the lounge chair next to her. I watched her closely this morning by our sliding glass door, very interesting person, I thought. She had a very nice figure, great face and very smooth skin. She gave me a slight smile of approval and continued reading her book.

Next to her was an older fella that was also reading. I figured that he must be her husband. I remembered seeing him with her earlier. She was wearing a very small bikini and had undone the top so she wouldn't have the tan lines. The way the furniture was set up, side by side, we were inches from each other and I could feel the sensual tension building between us. Every once in a while she would make eye contact and smile at me. I rolled over on my stomach and moved in a little closer. The man next to her had his nose buried in his book and was completely unaware of what was going on between the two of us. She put her book on her chest and turned her head towards me and smiled again. She then turned over on her stomach. I was on my belly, so when she moved she was eye to eye with me. Staring and smiling, she knew I was very turned on to her. She seemed to remember me and had this mischievous look on her face, unconcerned about the person next to her. The chances we were taking just seemed to make everything that much more exciting. She would tug on her top, and pull it down on the opposite side (facing her husband), only to reveal more of her breast on my side. I could have continued to play this game for hours, but decided to go and find something else to do. I remembered it may be time to meet Peggy. I gave her a big smile, pulled out my room key as I got up and gathered my towel. I had decided my last move, and placed my hand near her face and made sure she got a good look at my room number, figuring the next move would be hers, and I left.

    I was beginning to realize how romantic Acapulco is. Love is in the air, it's magical. There's something about the climate, warm, very soothing to the skin. It's very sensual, the sunshine, that's it, I thought. The latitude and longitude, the position near the equator, Acapulco must be so perfect it has this effect on everyone, that's it, that's why everyone is so approachable. Well anyway, the women were all smiles, and seemed to be very turned on everywhere I looked. I went up to the bar and sat down next to this foxy lady. After striking up a conversation with her, she seemed vaguely familiar. She asked me if I remembered meeting her the night before. She was quizzing me, I have to think fast. It all came to me at once, Peggy, your Peggy's mother. Very good, you know you're very good, she said, yes, we met at the Salsa club. This was her way of sizing me up. Just then her husband, (who wasn't at the Salsa club and I hadn't met) walked up with Peggy and her sister. Everyone was introduced to me by Peggy, as her dad invited me to join them at a nearby table for a drink and some conversation. Her family accepted me into their circle immediately. Peggy told me that they were from New York and that she was graduating from high school in May. Peggy starts college in New Jersey next semester. We are so proud. She's earned a scholarship, and with her grants will get a full ride, mother said proudly. I was very impressed. Her dad smiled, and asked me where I was from? San Antonio, I said. What part of Mexico is that in, he asked? I laughed and told him it was in Texas. They asked me if everyone in Texas rode horses. It depends on what part of Texas you're from I said.

Texas is a big state and in some ranching communities they do. San Antonio is a big city, and we use cars, I chuckled. Not knowing anything about Texas in those days, people just assumed everyone still rode horses. It was still a myth to people in the northeast like these folks. They seemed to really like me. And soon Peggy and I were off to the pool. We hit it off very well, and I was so happy to have someone to hang out with other than Jeff and Sandy. She was very down to earth. We had an immediate connection. It was as if I had known her a long time. We were an item right away. Later, we strolled on the beach holding hands, talking. As sunset was approaching, we sat on the beach and kissed for the first time. I asked if she would meet me later. My family and I are all going to the dinner buffet and after that dancing. Why don't you meet us at the buffet and have dinner with us about 8:30 PM. It's a date, I said without hesitation. I walked her to the elevator and she asked me to accompany her all the way to her room, so I would know where they were staying. I gave her one last kiss, and she went in.

When I got back to our room, I told them about Peggy. It's about time you met someone, Jeff chuckled. I was beginning to think you were gay. I didn't think twice about his comment as I headed for the shower. As I showered, I wondered what to do to kill time till 8:30 that evening before meeting up with Peggy, seeing how it was only 7 PM. As I exited the bathroom, there was a knock on the door. Since we weren't expecting anyone, I guessed maybe, room service? Wearing only my very large white hotel towel, I opened the door to reveal a sweet surprise. It was the older woman from the sundeck still in her bikini, with a large white hotel towel draped around her waist. I quickly grabbed her by the hand and pulled her into our room and locked the door. She hugged me, and I noticed she had a lot of sand on her feet and one of her legs. I mentioned I had just showered and she could be next. I quickly take her hand, and without any hesitation move towards the bathroom area. She kissed me wildly as I removed her towel. I squeezed her tightly, and proceeded to remove her top. She quickly pulled at my towel and went down on me. We had the best shower sex of my young life. We finished and exited only wearing our towels. It was very obvious she wasn't a shy person. Just then I realized I didn't even know her name. I whispered in her ear and she softly spoke the answer in mine, Melody, she whispered. The brush of her lips on my ear was so arousing I felt like I was ready for round two. She obviously stayed ready. So mature, and confident, she seems to know what she wants. As we approach the bedroom, Sandy and Jeff were still completely under the covers. Suddenly Jeff, to my embarrassment, says, it's about time you get laid, you horny little bastard. I thought you two were asleep. I tried to play it off. Melody just grinned and gave me a peck on the lips as I began the introductions. Sandy got out of bed wearing only a small pair of panties and said you all look so comfy I think I'll shower and grab a towel too. We'll just have a toga party, what do you think Jeff? I'm game, I'll shower next. I poured drinks. Jeff began to roll a joint. Melody mentioned she loved to smoke. Jeff was moving fast, fumbling the joint and picking it up off the carpeted floor handing it quickly to Melody. Jeff pulled out his lighter and she took a few puffs and said, it's been awhile, my husband is straight. She was probably about the same age as Jeff, I'm guessing maybe about 33 years old. Jeff was being very attentive towards Melody, she was eating it up. The attention from Jeff, that is. They had some chemistry going very quickly, I could tell. They actually make quite a couple, I pictured. In the back of my mind, I imagined Sandy alone with me as an item quite possibly sooner than later. I hoped this could be the break. I dreamed up an elaborate scenario and quickly fantasized being with Sandy, alone, finally. She didn't know that was my ultimate goal for this whole trip, the rest is pieces of the puzzle that lead me to Sandy. Well anyway, Sandy gets out of the shower and joins us. We are in the living area with a couch and loveseat, and are seated on the bar stools at the bar with drinks in hand. With the curtains drawn to the poolside patio and bar, the view was so beautiful and so were the women. Sandy does as promised, and appears to be just in the hotel terrycloth towel. Sandy satisfies my curiosity with a bold statement, yes, I am only in a towel. Sandy was smiling from ear to ear, we all were. The look on her face was so innocent. Sandy suggests to Jeff to shower and join the toga party. Jeff didn't need any encouragement, as he headed for the shower. I rolled a big fat joint and passed it to Melody, which in turn she passed to Sandy and so forth. It didn't take long for Jeff to reappear in full Togo party mode. He was ready to party. The music was turned up and we all danced to some Mexican music we found on a pretty good Mexican rock station. Mix in some oldies in English as well, and we all danced. We switched partners, right in time for a slow song. I was in heaven with my dream come true. Sandy felt so good I could hardly stand it. Her perfume scent gave me an instant erection, and she felt it when I pressed against her hard. Jeff and Melody were moving along in the same direction, and were soon kissing. So of course, I kissed Sandy, French, for the first time. I knew what was happening, I just couldn't believe it. Sandy grabbed my hand and led me to my bed. We made out like school kids. Jeff and Melody went to the other queen size bed. We watched some television and talked about the next day. Melody had to leave and accepted a date with Jeff. As she was leaving, saying her goodbyes, the last thing she said was, see you tomorrow at noon, Jeff. I said adios, and gave her a big kiss of gratitude and Jeff a big smile of approval. I was so excited, that meant I would have Sandy all to myself, the next day. There I go dreaming again. I cleaned up the bar, got dressed and left for my dinner date at 8:30 with Peggy.

I showed up on time and joined Peggy and her family for dinner. The whole evening was nicely chaperoned by her parents and sister, and younger brother, but I was rather enjoying something different for a change. It was a courtship kind of feeling in a fast-paced mode, but nonetheless I was thrilled by all the attention. These people were genuinely very nice and accepting of me. I was being tested and quizzed a little by the family but felt quite accepted and included in their little circle of life. After dinner and dancing, and with the approval of her parents and family, we were finally left all alone at the club. Quite frankly, I was enjoying both the mom and sister. They were both so beautiful and friendly. I actually danced with both of them, even some slow songs and could feel the attraction was mutual with both of them. I was careful not to go too far with those antics, because I was really falling hard for Peggy. She was the prettiest of all three of the girls.

We drank, kissed and felt each other out right there in the corner booth of the club. I was on my best behavior actually. I had been so satisfied earlier that I really held back on purpose, and wanted it to be so special with Peggy. I definitely wasn't in any hurry to get into anything heavy, for that night anyway. I guess she felt like waiting to get to know me a little better, which I found cool. Peggy was not easy, and I liked that, especially knowing we might never see each other again after Acapulco. I walked her to her room. After some heavy petting in the hallway, we made a date for the next evening at 7 PM. knowing that the next afternoon might be my lucky day. If things work out for me, Jeff will keep his date with Melody and I could be with Sandy at that opportune time. On the way back to my room, I thought, what's the hurry? I've got a few more days to get to know Peggy. The next day, I slept in. When I awoke, Sandy was in Jeff's arms in bed, both still asleep, they were positioned the same way every morning. They always slept a lot later than I. They were taking a lot of pills, Black mollies which are uppers, during the day, and early evening, and then Tuinal, also known as Christmas trees, which are downers, to get to bed and crash. So when they slept, it was deep and long sleep. My heart was racing with anticipation, I was very nervous. It was because I wanted to be with Sandy alone, that afternoon so bad. I also wanted to see Peggy, but Sandy was first, then Peggy later that night. Remember I'm a young man with plenty of desire.

I was observing them in bed. They look so out of it, Sandy was exposed as usual. She's trim at the waist, washboard abs, not an ounce of fat on her body. Her breasts are very large, upright, turned up shape, no sagging either. Super nice mushroom cap type nipples too, the kind very young and lucky girls have. Somehow I didn't really think about the age thing, she's sixteen, seventeen, I think she's legal, oh well I thought, we're in Mexico anyway. Different laws maybe? I don't know the laws here. I was very much attracted and infatuated with this beautiful young lady. She did not act, look or carry herself like a minor. I was in no position to really care.

I decided to shower, and remained optimistic, my dream fantasy may happen! When I finished getting ready, I stepped out of the room via the sliding glass door, and intentionally left it open so some of the pool activity sounds, or the wind or something, anything, would maybe wake them. I watched from right outside the glass sliding doors, curtains just slightly drawn, so maybe even the bright sunlight might awaken them from their deep slumber. I had to be careful as not to annoy, Jeff, for that would be a big mistake. It was a good move, something woke Sandy and somehow she actually got out of bed, and that woke Jeff. Yes, yes, I thought, as I quickly got out of sight, a few steps closer toward the pool. The next thing I hear is Jeff's voice. I could not believe my ears. Good morning, (he was in a good mood, I could tell by the tone of his voice), order us three frozen margaritas quick, and get in here. I scurried to the bar and placed my order, and thought, time is running out, Jeff's got to keep his noon date with Melody. I could only keep my fingers crossed he would actually remember. I signed the check for the margaritas and quickly reentered the hotel suite. I think Sandy read my emotions almost immediately. I passed out the drinks and Jeff headed for the bathroom and quickly closed the door. What's up with you, she asked? I mentioned Jeff's noon date with Melody. Sandy just smiled, and said for me not to worry. He mentioned it about three times while he was pounding me from behind last night. I think he was fantasizing being with her while he was doing me. Sandy seemed quite alright with the way the day was starting out. You know, for her age, Sandy was quite smart and pretty coolheaded, I thought. Jeff came out, toothbrush in his mouth and smiled, yeah yes, I'm going to meet Melody. He couldn't have heard our conversation but quickly let me know he knew what was going on and that he was cool with everything too. Sandy wants to be alone with you too, he said with a grin. I felt a bit of relief, but could hardly believe what he was saying. He was actually giving us his blessing. It was almost too good to be true. Sandy jumped in the shower next. Jeff got dressed and promised he would not be back before 6 PM for his pills and finished combing his hair. He was very anxious to see Melody, I could tell, which was a good thing for me. Jeff made his move towards the door, turned and smiled. I walked toward him and he extended his hand and reached out to shake my hand and said enjoy, as he left the suite. I thought about what had just happened, and had some realizations. We have a verbal contract for the next six hours. I had actually sealed the deal with a handshake of approval. I relaxed and began anticipating what was about to transpire for the rest of my precious time alone with Sandy. She was still in the shower, my heart raced and fluttered and probably skipped a beat or two, just thinking about the long awaited dream come true. Not only is the next six hours the most satisfying sexual encounter of my life, but believe it or not what I'm about to describe turns out to be a learning and very educational experience. I'm going to tell you in detail, of how a 17-year-old girl showed me something that I had never experienced or even actually ever heard of. Something, that even to this day, really and truly never gets mentioned or even brought up in, conversation. It doesn't make sense. Girls, women of all ages should be ashamed of not using, practicing, what this little teenage girl showed me.

Let me go back where I left off, Sandy's still in the shower. When Sandy finally came out of the bathroom, my eyes just couldn't believe what I seeing. Sandy was dressed to the nines, but only in lingerie. Turns out she was just as hopped up about being alone with me, maybe even more, than I could ever have imagined. She looked me straight in the eye and proclaimed she wanted me from the minute she saw me in that old pool hall. I've never had a Latino, ever. I hear Latin lovers are so hot and can go on forever, show me, please, please, please, she said as she approached. I was frozen stiff. I hadn't blinked, much less moved. I was getting quite stiff in the other department too! We hugged for a few seconds, I wanted to enjoy that particular moment, for all eternity, she looked so good, right out of Playboy magazine, Wow!! . She reached for my waist and slowly removed my swim suit. Her face reaching penis level, her mouth began to work some magic. This writing is not rated X, so I'll try to cut to the chase and explain what I learned the best way I can. The rest of the six hours is more of the same and very repetitive, almost programmed, natural and healthy. Darn right, good sex. I'd better leave a little to the imagination. So I don't want to bore you with the usual sex stuff, anyway, back to the lesson at hand.

"Vagina 101", I'll call it. It turns out Sandy had two sets of magic... Lips! As we lay in bed during my first penetration, I felt something going on, I had never experienced before. Sandy was doing something with her vagina. It felt incredible, sucking, pulling, holding onto my manhood. It just got stronger and stronger, the suction was a little strange but was the most wonderful throbbing sensation my penis had ever felt. Sandy remained motionless on the outside, just laying on her back, with an emotionless expression on her face, all the work was inside her vagina. It was total magic, for me.

My father had always taught me to practice safe sex. He had explained common law marriage, living with girls, women, and pregnancy. He gave me my first box of condoms. He explained all about sexually transmitted diseases and the risks of not wearing a condom. He went on to explain that, of course, sometimes you would not always wear the condom and needed to pull out of the vagina to climax.

Well, at this particular moment, pulling out seemed impossible. It was as if her vagina muscles would not have any part of letting go, not that I really wanted to anyway. The suction and pulling was tightening as if the muscles had a mind of their own and knew I was about to reach an orgasm. Sandy whispered in my ear and said, relax, I'm on birth control pills. My rhythm continued for a few more thrusts of this new experience, and I decided to try and hold back my explosion. No such luck, it came on hard and fast, it was the most explosive orgasm I had ever experienced. With every contraction I gushed, my orgasm seemed to go on forever, and ever. The sensation was very exotic, and erotic. It was like vacuum type suction. Whoosh, whoosh, whoosh, it continued, definitely the longest and most intense orgasm of my young life by far. The closest to male multiple orgasms I had ever experienced.

Sandy went on to explain, it was something she had learned as a young girl out of a book. My reaction, my first thought, I wish more women would read that book or article because it's never been done to me before. Sandy laughed and continued she didn't even miss a stride. Now I knew why Jeff hardly ever left Sandy's side. I'm sure Jeff was afraid to lose her to a younger man, or any man. She's literally the golden goose of sex, as far as I'm concerned. I was very curious and asked Sandy if she could explain how the procedure worked. Well if you must know, I didn't really think it was such a big deal, she said. I presumed that all women knew how to perform this way, it's really quite natural. Heaven's no, I replied. It starts in your mind. She went on, using a lot of concentration actually. Then you use your muscles, well your vagina muscles. I think the book referred to them as Pubococcygeus (PC) muscles. Also later commonly referred to as Kegel muscles, she explained. Kegel muscles let me write that down, I need to look that up in the dictionary, not really, just kidding. I thought to myself, not a bad idea, I think I really will. I'm sorry, go on. Well, you lay on your back, she continued, and work out the inner muscles of the vagina or Kegel muscles, you know, just like exercising any muscle. Multiple set of repetition, if you will. Tighten, loosen. Tighten, loosen, and so on. The muscles get stronger and stronger, the more you exercise, just like any other muscle in your body. Men have Kegel muscles too. With lots of exercise, and of course, lots of sex, you can really get to be quite consistent and this leads to lots of pleasure for the male partner. And of course, making my partner happy makes me happy. To say the least, I was very impressed, for her age, she was very sophisticated in her sexual knowledge. To Sandy, It seemed very natural, almost wholesome, like it was her duty as a woman. I wish all women were like you, Sandy, I said. Wow, that would be incredible, wow.

Personally to this day I've always wondered why no one ever talks about the Kegel muscles. Really, you never even hear about the wonderful built in sex tool that all women have. What comes to mind, and I hope I am not sounding chauvinistic, but, I guess women are either undereducated on the subject, or just plain too lazy to perform this for their man. Now, ladies, girls don't get mad at me, it's just my opinion. Please consider learning.

That experience led to one of my nicknames, actually my favorite early 70's, (Doctor). A friend at the same bar (he's deceased now). May he rest in peace, called me Doctor one day as we shared some conversation at the bar. I don't usually kiss and tell, but I had to brag about my sexual experience with Sandy. I was flattered by his comment and felt a bit complemented by his reference. I do come from an intelligent family. My sister is a Doctor. He called me Doctor throughout our conversation over and over and it just stuck with me after I left the pool hall. From then on, I would call friends, Doctor, I noticed, like myself, the title made people think, react and then naturally they always smiled with approval. Before long, people were always calling me Doctor so naturally, with this new sexual experience, and being called Doctor, I accepted the new nickname with pride. Next, I created my new pseudonym (pen name). Someday I thought I would write under the name Doctor. Every once in a while I would tell the story about Sandy and the guys, even the ladies, ate it up. People always seemed very curious to learn from my sexual experience with Sandy, especially, the girls. Most of the ladies wanted to know the secrets of the Kegel muscles. So I obliged. I became obsessed with this new knowledge and made up my mind up that I would write about the muscles and inform all women and the world. I seriously thought it was a great motivator and worthwhile topic of discussion. I took down a few notes and figured I would continue to write the article later, as I always do. I've been writing since the 60s, and always date and sign my writings. This book or novel "Acapulco" is something I wrote in 2002, as a movie script, or a chapter in my autobiographical writings for when I retire. Or my autobiography, but I decided the original twenty five page article was worth rewriting. I've decided to rewrite all of my chapters and turn each one into novels. Especially if "Acapulco", works for me, will see. The year was 1971 and I'd only written a few short stories, songs, and poems, but I realized how much I loved to write. I can go back to past experiences and remember with great detail what transpired. Then I put it on paper, and write a story. I only write when I get inspired. I play guitar, try to sing and love to be a part of a band or drama group. When I do get inspired, I grab a pen or pencil and take notes. It starts out, slow and easy, then it either picks up quickly, or the inspiration leaves my train of thought. You just never really know. Then I go back over it and rewrite, either right then and there, or I put it in a folder to keep on file with the rest of my writings. Most of the time I leave it in its original form, first thought, usually, the right thought. I do have somewhat of an autobiographical memory. The ability to go back in time, to a specific date, any given personal experience is deep down in my memory vault. I usually get a visual picture and its starts to run in my mind, like an old film projector, in middle school. This novel "Acapulco", has a very good message for any teenager growing up anywhere in the world. It will open their eyes, and minds to the fact that things, and people, are not always what we perceive them to be. Do not judge a book by its cover.

Sandy and I awoke in each other's arms and looked simultaneously at the clock on the wall. We both had the same thought in mind, anticipating Jeff's return. In the back of my mind, I immediately thought of my date with Peggy that evening at 8:30. Sandy and I showered together and could not get enough of each other. We dressed just in time for the opening of the door and the reappearance of Jeff. Jeff was alone and sported a great big smile. Melody was the best sex I've had in a long time, Jeff exclaimed. To my surprise, Sandy looked a little jealous, but played it off by putting her arm around my waist and saying that her Latin lover's manhood was much larger than his, and that I was the best, hottest, lover she had ever had.

With that statement everyone was all smiles, including me, it appeared the afternoon had been a totally gratifying sexual experience for both couples. I exited the suite quickly and headed for the main pool and bar area for my much anticipated date with Peggy, ah, right on time.

The next few days I spent most of my time with Peggy. We were together day and night. Jeff and Sandy were doing their thing, and I was doing mine. They were spending a lot of time in the room. This is where it appeared they were the happiest, just getting stoned all the time, and having a lot of sex. It seemed to me they were very content on just being with each other and wasted on those pills. Jeff was calling in room service quite a bit, and they hardly left the room for days on end.

Most evenings Peggy's family ended up at the Salsa club for drinks. That's where we always ended our nights together. This night would be different for it was there last night in Acapulco. They would be leaving in the morning. We danced, exchanged addresses and phone numbers and couldn't believe how fast the days had gone by. Her family was ready to call it a night, and was about to leave. Peggy got permission to stay, and promised her dad and mom she'd be up in about an hour. Her parents were very cool. I thanked them for everything and told them I was looking forward to seeing them again sometime, and said goodbye. We danced a slow song and as I held her tight, asked her if she wanted to come up to my room? She kissed me on the lips, and seemed to be shaking or kind of trembling with anticipation. On the way up the elevator, I explained Jeff and Sandy would probably be asleep. She didn't mind at all, and needed no convincing. She seemed to be as eager as I was. When we got to the room, it was pitch black, very, very dark. Just enough moonlight through the partially opened drapery, to see that they were passed out, probably on downers. I slowly undress her. She had the smoothest skin and I quickly kissed her neck and shoulders working my way down to her small but firm breasts. I quickly inserted one finger in her vagina. This is protocol for me, before going down under, if you know what I mean. I've got to get a good sense of what it's going to taste like before taking the plunge. I've learned that once you go down it's going to be awhile before she lets you get back out, leg lock or not. Peggy smells terrific, I thought, as I continued my decent toward her pussy. As I began to eat her out, I noticed Sandy was now apparently awake and very exposed which of course turned me on even more. Sandy was well aware of what was going on and began her own show of gratitude for our performance. We made eye contact and both smiled. Peggy seemed oblivious, hadn't noticed, or just didn't really care one way or another, she was in Heaven anyway. Sandy began to play with herself, as I continued my oral attack on Peggy. We made love passionately for about an hour. Afterwards, as I held her in my arms, she asked me if I would meet them in the lobby the next morning to see her one last time. Of course, I said, it would be my pleasure. They had been super cool to me, I wouldn't miss saying bye to you and your family for the world, I said, as I kissed her long and hard knowing it may be our last passionate kiss for a long while, I really liked Peggy. We dressed and headed out the door for the elevators. Hand in hand it was very romantic. I walked her all the way to her room, and kissed her goodnight. See you in the morning, and gave her one last hug and kiss, before finally leaving. I meant every word, I was being sincere.

The next morning, Peggy was very excited to see me waiting for her in the lobby. She gave me a huge reception, kisses, hugs and laughter. As we walked, holding hands, her parents smiled with approval. As if previously discussed, I was asked if I would join them for our last and parting meal. After our meal we all headed back to the lobby. The valet had their luggage on a cart, next to the front desk. Peggy's father signed off on the invoice, and we all followed him and the valet person out the front door. I gave her one last kiss, as we promised each other we'd stay in touch. They jumped in a cab and were off to the airport.

After Peggy's cab was out of sight I headed for our room. Jeff and Sandy were still laid out as usual. They'd called in room service and had already had breakfast. Sandy was told to roll some joints and got out of bed totally nude. I never tired of seeing her body. It was total perfection, not an ounce of fat. She reached for a towel and asked me if Peggy had left? Staring at her beautiful body I said yes. Jeff said not to worry, assuring me that Sandy would take care of me later that night. We all laughed. Sandy and I looked at each other with the same anticipated notion, the sooner the better, we were hot for each other right now, especially after last night's session with Peggy, Sandy was grinning from ear to ear. I knew that she had been watching the whole time I was with Peggy. She was hot to trot with me, and I knew it. And I truly felt Jeff would share Sandy from that moment on. I wanted Sandy from the minute I first laid eyes on her. I couldn't get enough of her ever I thought. I think I love her. She was probably the deciding factor which convinced me to come on this trip in the first place. I didn't really know whether it was a big con from the beginning to get me to come or if she really liked me. But now I truly believe she does like me, but still used me for their safe passage across the Mexican border. Jeff and Sandy were both very good actors, cons, if you will. They were a good team. It was very hard to read them, much less understand them. They were very unpredictable. We smoked some pot and drank some coronas. Sandy jumped into the shower. During our conversation, Jeff asked if I had been down to the hotel spa. No, I didn't even know the hotel had one. He asked if I would like to join them for the full spa treatment. I quickly said, yes. I've never experienced a spa. I'm dressed and ready to go. After Jeff dressed, we went down to an area of the hotel I hadn't seen. This hotel had everything. Now that I think about it, we really never left the hotel again. We had not left the hotel since the day we went for a drive and bought our swimsuits. We didn't have to, everything was right here at our convenience. I had never experienced this luxurious type of five Star Hotel. These giant hotels were set up so you wouldn't leave and spend your money elsewhere.

Chapter Seven

Oriental Express

They had everything under one roof. This floor, we had just reached, looked like the mall in San Antonio, shops galore. We went into the jewelry shop, and Jeff bought Sandy a very nice gold necklace. He even offered to buy me something, but I declined. I wasn't much for flashy jewelry, nor had I really ever owned any to speak of. Next, we headed for some clothing shops and browsed around. Sandy picked out a new, tiny, itsy-bitsy bikini. She tried it on, and came out modeling the swimsuit. She was so hot. Everyone in the shop noticed her talent. Even the sales girl smiled. After Jeff signed for the merchandise, we headed out the door and down a flight of steps, and ended up in the workout area of the spa. Let's get a massage, Jeff said. I had never had one before, but when I saw the women who were ready to give it, I was game. All three of us went behind some partitions, and stripped off our clothing. The only thing around was a large white terrycloth hotel towel which I wrapped around my waist. It was on a small table next to a massage table with a dimly lit Palm tree looking lamp on the nightstand. The room lighting was dim and very sensual and romantic. The aroma of incense and body lotion or some type of cream fragrance, was in the air and immediately aroused my sexual aura and I was about to find out why. Appearing from behind a linen type, almost see through curtain I could see the silhouette of a woman approaching, to my surprise, it was a very, very young looking Asian girl. My name is Gigi Chow she said. Gigi appeared to be about 13 or 14 years old, but said she was 16. The whole time, this conversation is in Spanish of course. Gigi speaks some English, and speaks fluent Chinese around her mom and aunt at the house, she mentions. Turns out, she explains, she's half Mexican and half Chinese. I found her very attractive and the

Asian look and her beautiful smile made me feel appreciated. Gigi was wearing a white terrycloth hotel type robe tied at the waist with a pink and gold sash belt. The robe was short and very sexy. She wore some little sandals on her tiny feet that had the house slipper appearance, very nice touch, I thought, they look very sexy and very comfortable. Gigi looked very relaxed and eager to please. She was all smiles and projected lots of energy as she rubbed some lotion in her palms. Ne ho ma? She said, in Chinese. How are you? Thank you for coming in for a massage today. It's been a very slow day and I have been bored all morning. You are welcome I said, glad to be here, my name is Tony. She came over and grabbed me by my hand and led me over to the massage table. I laid down flat on my stomach. I was a bit nervous, but I was very excited. The thought of one whole hour with this little girl gave me a thrill. Gigi went on to flatter me by saying how glad she was to see someone in her age group. Mostly I get fat older men. She laughed, I smiled with approval. She immediately loosened the towel from around my waist and just left it loosely over my buttocks. Gigi next asked me if it would be all right for her to remove her robe, it's pretty hot down here in the basement, she said. I smiled, and could not believe my ears. Perfect, I thought today's my lucky day. She reached for the body lotion rubbed her hands together and started working her magic, it was incredible. I was in heaven. She started at my feet actually, and worked her way up my legs. By the time she got to my thighs, I was throbbing in delight. I am sure it was obvious to the masseuse who quickly asked, first time for massage? Yes, I answered in a shuddering, stuttering kind of way, yes, yes. Gigi mentioned it happened all the time, and we change the sheets very often too, she smiled and said. Right there and then with that statement I knew she was okay with the hard on and me being very turned on, green light, I was almost shaking. She went over the midsection and my back quickly and reached up high to my shoulders. Ah, ah, I murmured in a soft moan. Oh, I moaned again. You like, she asked? Gigi was very short, tiny, very petite, small frame, making her appearance very childlike which aroused me to the max. Gigi was not wearing much, tiny bikini panties and a lace bra, covered only by a sheer see through Teddy like very short outfit. I hadn't gotten a very good look at her body since she had been working on my lower torso. As she tiptoed and started on my shoulders, she was very close to my face. What a beautiful body, I thought. She continued working on my neck and shoulders, and as she did, she began to press her pelvic area into my arm and elbow. There was this full-length mirror up against the wall and I could see her body from behind in the reflection. What a beautiful sight. The placement of the mirror was ingenious. She began to lower her breasts so that they would rub on my back as she massaged my neck and shoulder areas. When she leaned far enough forward you could also see her firm breasts. They were very nice for her size and age. She asked me to turn over on my back, and went back down to my legs. She worked her way from my feet, legs, and upper thighs, rather quickly and on her way up she slightly moved the towel and left me fully exposed. Gigi reached for more cream, and asked if I wanted a massage here too? As she looked at my erect penis, I said, oh yes please, as she placed her little hands around my rather large hard on. I won't get into details about the rest of the session, but you know, I had a very happy ending. Gigi and I hit it off so well. I felt confident enough to ask her to meet me in front of the hotel after work that same day. Gigi explained her schedule for that evening made it difficult for today. She also said she had to ask her mom for permission to go out with any young man. You'll have to meet my mom, Mona, before she approves anything with you. Gigi went on to explain that her mother was also a masseuse and cocktail waitress for the hotel and that she worked the early shift on the beach in front of our hotel serving drinks. Perfect I said, how about early tomorrow. I'll be having a drink on the beach, looking for your mom and waiting for you, it's a date, right? How's that sound? You really will meet my mom? Of course I will. I really like you a lot, I said. That's nice. She said most guys don't want to do it. Well I am not most guys.

It would be my pleasure, remember, I'm from Texas, we're gentleman back home and in Acapulco. Now, is it a date? I can't promise, but I'll try my best, Gigi said. That's good enough for me. Hopefully I'll see you tomorrow, see you later and I left. It was great, very relaxing, something I had never experienced. I sat on a very comfortable leather couch while I waited for Jeff and Sandy to finish their sessions. I thought about the next morning with great anticipation, hoping Gigi's mom, Mona, would be somewhat understanding and approve of our date. It wasn't long before they appeared at the exit. As we left the spa area, I thought, that was the most pleasurable and quickest hour I have ever had in my entire young life. Jeff put his arm around my shoulder and I reached my arm around Sandy's shoulder and we were off like the three musketeers. The beauty salon is the next, follow me, Sandy said. I liked my hair long, but accepted a trim anyway. We looked and felt great with our new hairstyles. Showers and hot tubs are next, Jeff said, with a grin. Jeff knew the good life. This was all very new to me. At that moment, I thought to myself, Jeff must be richer than I thought. Afterwards we head over to the lunch buffet. We were tired and hungry, I was starving. That afternoon I truly missed being with Peggy, but had really enjoyed hanging out with Sandy and Jeff. We headed for the beach. After lunch, I realized they were much braver than I, as Sandy reached for a parachute Jeff handed her to prepare for parasailing. Being pulled by a speedboat and flying high above the Bay with a parachute on your back, seems a little dangerous to me, I'll pass, as I watched Jeff strap on his parachute to go next. It was a lot of fun watching them, but I never really built up the courage or really even gave it a second thought. We hung out on the beach pretty much the entire afternoon. Once back in the room, we started to party again, and I got pretty high quickly. The previous days I had spent with Peggy, I had remained straight, so the smoke hit me pretty hard. We stayed in the room that night and watched TV. Jeff called room service and, ordered some club sandwiches and French fries. Shortly after dinner Sandy rolled us a joint and, Jeff asked Sandy to do a striptease type of dance for us. I turned on the clock radio for some music and instant ambience, it worked. The gyration of her hips started slowly and very seductively. I'm very tired, so only one song, she announced. She had kind of a Hawaiian belly dance type of rhythm going, but looked very sexy. She quickly removed her blouse, skirt, and bra and finally her panties, she was totally nude very quickly. She jumped under the covers and said, good night.

The next morning, I awoke about 8 a.m. to find the door to the bathroom wide opened, and Sandy's reflection in the mirror stark naked looking right at me with a big smile on her face. I looked over to the other bed (side-by-side queen size beds) and saw that Jeff was still asleep. I watched as she turned on the water to the shower. Just as she was stepping in, she turned and motioned with her finger, to join her. Her finger continued to move ever so demanding, my eyes transfixed on the index, I was in a trance, I obliged immediately. I quickly removed my bikini briefs and got in the shower with Sandy, but not before locking both hall and bathroom doors. I was getting a little braver as the days went on. I got to know Jeff's routine pretty well and felt quite certain he wouldn't wake seeing how he always slept past noon. Nonetheless the doors were both locked and I figured what the hell, she's worth it. Sandy reached for a razor and a bar of soap. She began to lather her pubic area, as she passed me the razor. She wanted me to shave her pubic hair into a heart shaped love nest. I was game, but had no experience. I'm willing to learn, I fired back. It was very exciting, and I could tell she was really enjoying my close contact with her vagina. At my age I had very little oral experience, but figured that was where this was leading, I was throbbing with excitement. I got my face really close and she lifted her leg over my shoulder and I dove in face first. I had to position her legs just right so I wouldn't drown. There was a lot of water, which made it rather interesting. I deep tongued her for a while till she shuttered, as I tightened my grip on her ass. Her legs wobbled, as she smiled gratefully, as to say, I really enjoyed that. Sandy reached for the soap and handed me the razor. I continued where I had left off. It began to take shape, it was rather easy. I caught on quickly. Before I knew it, I was done. The heart looked beautiful, and I was super aroused. I want something to remember you by for a while, Sandy said, licking her lips, and patting her new look. She went down to her knees, placed both hands on my manhood and kissed and sucked, all the while looking up at me with a huge smile. Next, she stood and guided me inside her heart shaped love nest. We had some great shower sex standing for a few more minutes and I reached a huge climax. We made out like the teenagers that we were. I usually don't kiss that much, but was genuinely enjoying it. Sandy seemed to really be into it. Maybe it was my small lips and fast tongue. I had been told many times in the past that I did wonders with my small lips, and that I was very good at kissing, by many a young lady. I shut the water off and quickly grabbed a towel. I was in a fast forward. Just thinking about Jeff in the next room was very scary. I closed the door behind me that separates the shower from the sink and toilet area quickly. I made sure to lock it from her side, just in case. I put my underwear back on, and wrapped the towel around my waist, as I peeped out carefully. The coast is clear, I made a B-line for my bed, and quickly got under the covers, and pretended to be asleep for a while just in case. Call me a little paranoid, that's O.K. Jeff was still asleep, passed out cold, like usual. He takes pills, downers, every night to help him sleep. We were done, and Jeff didn't know a thing about it, that's how I wanted it. Sandy, I believe, didn't really care one way or another. She wasn't a bit scared of Jeff. But I was most certainly being as careful as possible. Jeff had a very low threshold for anger, and violence. He was always taking downers before bed and would sleep heavily sedated every night and morning. Sandy and I began to enjoy lots of early morning escapades while Jeff was passed out. Sandy came out all innocent like, wearing a white hotel towel. She opened her arms, holding the towel stretched out like angel wings and said, I really like the heart and ran up to my bed, so I could kiss the heart, which I quickly did, seeing how Jeff was still passed out. Afterwards, she jumped back in bed with Jeff. I walked over and turned on the TV, adjusting the volume down low. As we both pretended to be waking for the day. It really didn't matter. That's what I was thinking. Seeing how Jeff was still asleep anyway. Sandy and I talked for a while and I tell her all about Gigi. She was very interested in all the facts about the time I spent with the masseuse. I mentioned that I was going to meet Gigi at around 10a.m. this very morning. Sandy really got enthusiastically excited for me. She wanted all the details. She said she wanted to meet her as quickly as I could introduce her. I promised I would if I could, and my imagination quickly flashed a beautiful picture of this wonderful threesome.

I put on my brand new Hawaiian swimsuit, and head to the beach. Arriving out in front of the hotel I come upon a vacant palapa, and claimed it for my own. The beach front was packed as usual. This is snow bird season, I had learned, all of the tourists were here this time of year every year, it's the winter break from school and the Christmas holiday season, it'll be packed till the New Year, I had heard. As I sat in the morning shade, I was looking for a waiter or waitress, so I could order a Bloody Mary. I always started my mornings in Acapulco with a Bloody Mary. I wasn't paying the tab or hotel bill anyway, why not live it up, not to worry, Jeff is super rich anyway, I always figured. Other mornings and days it was usually a waiter, but this morning, as it quickly was nearing 10 a.m. it was a beautiful waitress. She was wearing a nice swimsuit type outfit with a little vest, very sexy lady, I guess maybe, about 35 years old, and to my surprise looked a little Asian. I quickly asked if her name was Mona. Yes, she responded. By my daughter's description I thought it might be you, she answered. I'm Mona, you must be Tony? My pleasure, you're as beautiful as Gigi described. I looked deep into her eyes and wanted her so bad, I think she knew it. I quickly cooled my jets, realizing how much I really liked Gigi. I was starting to realize that love was in the air all the time in

Acapulco. I was always getting these great vibes from almost every female I came into contact with. I couldn't believe it. It's so true. Believe me. You would have to be here to feel and experience the sexual aroma in the air. Love is truly everywhere, something to do with the climate, and warm sunshine. Maybe it's just the mix of people, cultures, races and season. I am not sure, I cannot fully understand it, but I couldn't get enough of the climate. I want to live here for the rest of my life, in my dreams of course, if only in my dreams, I thought.

What will it be? I'll get you a drink while you wait. Assuring me that Gigi was on her way from the house. I'll have a Bloody Mary please. Mona suggested I try a Mimosa. You will really enjoy them in the morning, champagne and orange juice with a dash of cherry juice and a cherry, and it's on me. I'll try it! As she walked away, I noticed her body was very similar to Gigi's. I loved it, small, very petite and tanned. Mona soon returned with my drink and others on her tray to serve to the hotel guests. Enjoy, she said with a big smile of approval. I watched her swaying rear end as she turned and walked away looking back at me, while heading towards her other customers. You like what you see? I was startled by a beautiful soft voice behind me. It was Gigi, in an itsy-bitsy teeny red bikini, yes, I guess so. I hesitated to say, it's okay, it happens all the time. Everyone thinks we're sisters. Gigi noticed the look on my face and seemed to get a kick out of it. She sort of laughed. Your mom is the nicest. I really like her a lot. So does every boy I've ever met, but that's okay, we're housemates and best friends. We are very close. We're all we've got. Gigi went on to explain. My dad has been gone since I was 10, car accident. I'm really sorry for your loss. Thanks, now where's my drink, she said quickly, as to change the subject. I gave her mine, and she took a sip. I quickly grabbed her hand and held it tightly. I learned at a young age that girls really like that. A few minutes later, Mona returns with a large tray of appetizers, and a pitcher of Mimosas, and three glasses. She joined us and mentioned it was time for her break. We should enjoy the moment on the beach together, here's to you, Tony, she said. We got to know each other a little with the usual parent questions, where are you from? How old are you? How long are you staying in Acapulco? Everything seemed to go just fine with Mona, Gigi's mom. As she got up and picked up her tray. She seemed very happy with me and smiled with approval. As Mona left to return to her awaiting customers, Gigi kissed me on the cheek, and said we could make plans now for our next date. I hugged Gigi. She was so excited she jumped up with a leg lock around my waist, as we tumbled to the sand. We kissed and cuddled as we rolled around on a large beach towel in the sand. After getting totally covered with sand from head to toe, we headed for a swim in the Bay. The morning passed quickly, and we had so much fun. Later that afternoon Mona came back, it was time to go. Gigi joined her mom, and we said our goodbyes. I quickly invited them to the dinner buffet that evening at the hotel, my treat. Eight p.m. please, if possible. As they walked away, Mona turned and smiled, will see, she said.

Gigi kissed me on the cheek, and said goodbye. Then she whispered, room 311, I'll call your room. I'll be waiting. I grabbed my towel, and headed to the room for a nice cool shower.

It was about six p.m. and I was very surprised to find an empty hotel room. It was really a nice surprise. It was nice to have some time alone to gather my thoughts. I pulled out some postcards and began to write some loving words to my family. I really missed them. I had never been away this long, ever. This was my first Christmas away from home. I'm fine, love you, I miss you. See you soon, the regular son stuff. I went down to the lobby and found the mail slot near the front desk. In they went, as I let go of the postcards, down they went. I was somewhat relieved. I had been feeling rather guilty for waiting so long for some kind of communication with the folks, the family. Actually I felt, some fulfillment. It wasn't much, but I felt like I had accomplished some great task.

I was really excited and could hardly wait to see if Gigi and Mona would join me for dinner. I called the front desk and asked to borrow an iron so that I could press my pants. Luckily I had packed one pair of long pants, some decent looking slacks, very wrinkled, but new. I was in luck and I was promised the iron within the next 10 minutes. I had placed my new Hawaiian style shirt on a hanger in one of the closets. It appeared that it was ready to wear, no ironing needed. It was one of the gifts that Jeff had bought me. I was glad to have something nice and new to wear for the evening. I finished dressing and went down to the bar out by the main pool and buffet area. I found a spot available at the main bar, and pulled up a bar stool. The trio of Mexican musicians looked very similar, and familiar. Resembling the trio's I see in the Mexican restaurant Mi Tierra in the market square or Mercado in San Antonio, my hometown. They were very good and sang many old and familiar songs that I remember from my dad and mom's favorites. The bar was hopping and the servers were busy setting up the dinner buffet. I was starving. After my second frozen, top shelf Margarita, I looked around for a table near the food line. I was in luck and secured my position at a four top. A beautiful waitress appears and I mention that I'm expecting two more in my party. Of course, let me make it clear that throughout most of this writing we are speaking Spanish. I ordered a bottle of water and a Tecate beer with a dressed glass (salt and a lime), and asked if she would please start a tab for me, as I flashed my room key and number. She flashed a big smile, yes sir, right away.

It was 10 min. after 8:00, and I was really getting impatient and very hungry. I decided to help myself to a salad. I still had high hopes they would show. The food at our hotel was incredible. It's always fresh and tasty. In between bites, I felt a soft and gentle touch on my shoulder. I turned and saw two beautifully dressed and very sexy girls. Mona looked so young. You'd think they were sisters. Mona had done up her hair pulled back in a ponytail and bangs in the front. They were both dressed in similar Asian outfits, long silky dresses with a too die for slit on one side about to the knee, very classy, resembling twins. Gigi, you look incredible, and Mona, wow! They hugged me like a hero sandwich, as they joined me. I pulled out their chairs as to represent the gentleman that I am. I see chivalry is not dead in Texas, Mona remarks, I like that. I motioned for the waitress as she quickly took their order, drinks for everyone, I said, with excitement. Mona, to my delight, spoke up and suggested we order a pitcher of frozen Margaritas and three glasses, cool, I thought. We hit the buffet, enjoyed dinner and two pitchers of Margaritas, had some great conversation, and I suggested the Salsa club for our next stop. It was unanimous. I signed the bill, flashed my room key, like magic, a guy could get used to this, I thought. And we were off to the club for some dancing. We found a table near the dance floor.

We sat for a while and talked. Just getting to know Gigi and her mom Mona was very interesting conversation. A great fast song was next as the D J worked his magic. The three of us got up simultaneously, and headed for the dance floor. I was the luckiest guy in the club, two beautiful women. As we danced I noticed my watch and noticed how time flies when you're having fun. It was about 10:30 PM and we were going strong. I looked toward the door and to my surprise saw Sandy and Jeff walking in the club. They were dressed to the nine's. Sandy was in a short black dress with shiny silver trim and Jeff was wearing a handsome sports coat. They looked incredible. I could hardly believe my eyes, what a great couple. They shared a big smile as they approached us. You all look great, I said. We went shopping, you like? Sandy boasted. Yes, very much so, I said. These are my new friends, Mona, and Gigi, this is Sandy and Jeff. Immediately after the introduction, Sandy said, I've heard a lot about you Gigi, somebody really thinks you're super special, and I can see why. Pleased to meet you both, Jeff interrupted. Join us, please, as I directed everyone towards our table. Drinks are all on me tonight, Jeff announced proudly. Before long we were all on the dance floor having the time of our lives. After regrouping at our table, and some small talk, Jeff surprised us all by asking Mona to dance a slow song. Be careful, he's quite the lady's man, Sandy said, with her obvious approval. I considered myself quite the lady's man. Of course my style is completely different than Jeff's. He's much older and wiser than I, with much more experience. He's definitely a class act, and lots of money too. I'm young, but have the gift of gab, a very fast tongue. I have a convincing charm and have a few secrets I'd learned from having four sisters. All their girlfriend's conversations and things I would overhear truly help with inside info, if you get my drift. One of the most valuable lessons I had learned from a total stranger, a beautiful young girl, wise beyond her years, was a hard knock to the ego at a club in San Antonio, Texas where I live. Just in case I haven't mentioned Texas had for a few years lowered the drinking age to eighteen before changing it back to twenty one again a couple of years later. I had just met her that night, and had been working it hard, lots of dancing, three or four drinks in a row, a few bucks had been invested. I was in like Flint, so I thought. Everything was working for me. We were already seated in a corner booth, and were smooching, and talking about later, ah pay dirt. Somehow, my rap got so long, I was bored with it, so she began to speak about herself, and what she did and liked to do. I glanced to the left and then to the right, just basically, not paying attention to her, looking at other people, mostly the other girls. Well, she was not at all impressed, and stood up and proceeded to let me have it, her passion was truly impressive, I did pay attention to that part, and to this day, I'm glad I did. I lost her that night, but was given a life altering inside to what women expect and really demand from a man. You really should learn how to listen, she said, loudly, as she began to walk away. You need to learn how to listen, she repeated. I froze in my seat, I was speechless, no come back, no excuses, just embarrassment and silence. As she walked away I realized what she had meant, and it all came to me in a flash, in living color actually, clear as day, the message was there. Women want to be heard, and listened to especially after they've listened attentively to us. They want a sympathetic ear, some positive feedback, and that certain connection of being on the same page with whom they are about to take the relationship to the next level. Especially if you move along at the pace I was taking it, or about to take it when we would leave the club. She was smart. She knew what I was expecting. I had made it so obvious. I learned a lot from that reprimand. What a flash back. Anyway, back to the club and my story, making sure I was hanging on to every word Gigi or her mom, Mona, uttered I couldn't miss a vibe for it might mean missing a single message they would be portraying. Listening to women had become like second nature, it really works, they're like putty in my hands, just listen, and learn what they really want. They will let you know. Jeff and I took turns dancing with all three of the ladies. When it came time for me to dance with Mona my heart was racing, it was a fast song but we held hands and danced pretty close. The very next song was a slow melody and I could tell she was ready for my advancing arms around her waist. I held her tight and very close with both arms around her tiny waist. She kissed my ear and I got an instant erection, which she could feel right away. She smiled with approval and said you're a young stud aren't you. Be careful with Gigi she really likes you a lot, and so do I, I'm really looking forward to getting to know you better. My daughter is not at all jealous and neither am I. I held her tighter than ever, I pressed up against her so hard I nearly blew a nut right there on the dance floor, and she knew it. Save it for later, she said. Wow, I thought, I'm on such a roll with the ladies, I couldn't believe all the luck I was having, but after all, "Love is in the air" in Acapulco. I love this town. Pay special attention to Gigi and make her happy and you may get to me, Mona went on, vibrating her sweet lips on my right ear lobe, very erotically. Everything that went on between us on the dance floor seemed to go on unnoticed by Gigi and she didn't bat an eye. Mona winked as if to say, see, it's ok with my daughter. I started to imagine wild sex with first Gigi and then Mona, wow. My attention shifted back to Gigi, remembering what Mona had said. Back on the dance floor I seductively pulled Gigi closer and tighter while we danced a very slow song. She felt my bulge and asked if my heightened excitement was solely for her? I think some of it is for Mona, but I'm not jealous, she really likes you, I might just have to share you if you prove to be too much for me. I think we both want you, she said, as she began to tremble and shake just a little, like the girls in the catholic high school gymnasium dances used to do. She climaxed in her panties, I'm sure, I loved it. It felt like good old times, cheap thrills. Just like a school girl, she literally trembled with delight and shuttered again and again. I held her tight as I pressed my manhood between her legs. Her eyes rolled back and she kissed me. Dance with Mona please, I need to be excused, as she headed for the ladies room. My feelings for Gigi were sincere, so young, and beautiful. I was very attracted to her. I had never been with an Asian girl, and she had really pushed my sensual arousal buttons when she gave me that wonderful massage. When

I got back to the table I needed a bathroom break. Join us, Sandy said, we're munching on shrimp cocktail and some oysters. Help yourself. Jeff ordered another pitcher of Margaritas, as I left and Gigi returned. My turn, I'll be right back. Sandy licked her lips and appeared to be staring at my crotch. Physically still aroused I guess she noticed my bulge. Upon my return Sandy wanted in on some of the action. She motioned towards the dance floor. We talked as we dance. Sandy said she wanted to have a threesome with Gigi. Let me assure you Sandy, if and when I have sex with Gigi, if she's game, I'm willing to share. We walked back to the table hand in hand, and joined the others. The whole group was staring and smiling at Sandy and I, it was apparent Mona and Gigi really liked Sandy and Jeff, but mostly Sandy. Can you blame them, tall, young, built like a brick house. Mona mentioned it was getting late and that they should get going. Mona asked the waitress for a pen and a napkin and proceeded to draw us a map with the directions to their house. She insisted we come over for dinner and some fun the next evening, seven p.m. and be prompt, we don't like to be kept waiting, she exclaimed. We all confirmed and agreed we wouldn't miss it for the world. Mona told us it was a fifteen minute drive from our hotel. Simple enough, Jeff said. We all hugged and said our goodbyes. I insisted on walking them out to the parking garage and safely to their car. Gigi mentioned that I had been a total gentleman. You truly are Mona complemented, as I closed the car door. See you tomorrow. I assured them as they drove off. Getting back to our hotel room, Sandy and Jeff were quite happy with me, and were gleaming with anticipation for what the next evening could bring. We'll sleep late, and then go shopping for some goodies to show up with for the dinner party, Jeff said. Now, good night, I need my beauty sleep, Sandy said. Good night.

The next day came soon enough. We readied ourselves after just laying around all afternoon. After we were all dressed and ready to roll, we decided to go to a local mall and get some house warming gifts. It's very important we show up with a special gift for Mona, Jeff mentioned. Candy, flowers, a bottle of champagne, some sparkling wine, Sandy agreed. Sure, let's roll, I said excitedly.

The directions were simple enough, upon arriving atop a hillside home. It was beautifully landscaped as the gardener trimmed the rose bushes. We were definitely impressed. A two story Mexican style villa, with a second story terrace looking over Acapulco Bay and a pool, just like in the movies. And all that was what we could see from the driveway, at first glance, wow. I rang the doorbell. We were greeted at the door by a woman maybe fifty or fifty-five years old, hola, pasale, hi, come on in. Speaking mostly in Spanish, she said, I'm Maria, the housekeeper and cook, make yourselves at home the ladies will be down in a minute. Maria asked if she could help with the bags as Sandy and Maria headed to the kitchen. The house was not what I had expected. I had imagined a small humble home seeing how it was just the two of them, judging from what Gigi had told me. Boy was I wrong.

Welcome to our home, mi casa es su casa, Mona said. Gigi, shadowing closely behind her mother, (they were both dressed in very familiar white terry cloth robes), was carrying what appeared to be more robes. Take your shoes off and change into these please, the dressing rooms are this way, as she led us all down the hallway. This is really nice. Very sexy, very cool. Gigi just smiled as we disappeared to change. After reentering the living room, there were lots of warm hugs and kisses. Maria was more like family, as everyone was properly introduced by Mona. Maria was very petite and slender, very pretty for an older woman. She was definitely Asian and possessed a very sexy smile. Her face was smooth and wrinkle free, very happy type of person. Maria disappeared into the dressing room and returned looking hot. She also had changed into a white robe. Maria has very special hands, almost magical, Mona explained. She trained us both in the art of massage. Maria always helps out in every way around the house, she lives with us and is part of the family, Gigi explains. Turns out,

Maria is Mona's deceased husband's sister, and Gigi's aunt. When Mr. Chow, Mona's husband died (car accident, 5 years ago) she moved in their home to comfort and help them carry on with all the formalities of the funeral and burial proceedings and settling the family estate. That was five years ago, she never left and she took on some of the chores around the house it appears, seeing how she was dressed in a sexy maids outfit upon our arrival. That explains the large beautiful home. Mr. Chow was of Chinese decent and was a very successful import/export whole sale distributor. Looking around the décor was very Chinese, Mr. Chow specialized in hand painted porcelain vases and figurines.

We sat in the living room and snacked on appetizers. We sipped on wine and popped a bottle of champagne. Maria waited on us hand and foot, but you could tell she enjoyed every minute of it. Meeting new people was her joy, she explained, my pleasure, she responded, after I thanked her. She seemed to have a gleam in her eyes and was clearly infatuated with Jeff, which pleased me. Maybe she could entertain Jeff, which could give me more time with Gigi, and Sandy, and our dreamy threesome.

After some small talk, Gigi grabbed my hand and also reached over and took hold of Sandy's. Come with me, she said. Mona and Maria pulled Jeff off the couch, as we were led down a long corridor. We entered a large room filled with fitness equipment, complete with showers, a Jacuzzi, and steam room, hot dam, I thought. Off to the right were two massage tables side by side with a beautiful Chinese partition that served as privacy between the two tables. Jeff and I were instructed to lie down and get comfortable. The ladies disappeared for a few minutes and came back with warm body oil. Gigi and Sandy were going to service me. And of course, Mona and Maria were to take care of Jeff. Everyone appeared to be happy with the arrangement, I know I was. Oh my, four hands all over my body, I was in heaven. Jeff was mumbling something, but I couldn't make it out. I told him to keep it down, jokingly. Impossible, he said, as we all laughed.

The massage was a short one for it didn't take long for my happy ending. From the sound of it, Jeff was right there with me, blast off.

Next the steam room, Jacuzzi, and showers. Not a shy crowd, everyone seemed comfortable with all the nudity. Maria suggested dinner, seeing how she was roasting a chicken in the oven. I'm sure it's done, you hungry? After showering, we all meet in the dining room, please, Maria announced.

After a wonderful dinner, Mona put on some really romantic Mexican music and asked me to dance. We started it off and Jeff and Sandy joined in for a slow melody. Gigi winked at me as she disappeared into the kitchen with Maria. Then we switched partners, it was lots of fun and very sexy stuff. Gigi came back out just in time for a fast song and we all danced. After lots of dancing and drinks, Mona asked Maria to help her clear the dining room table. It's time to do the dishes, Maria agreed, as they headed for the kitchen. As soon as they disappeared into the kitchen, Jeff motioned for us to follow him out the sliding glass doors to the patio out by the pool. It was dark except for the beautiful moon light and the glimmering stars. Suddenly in a flash, a familiar smell of marijuana was in the night air. How sweet it is. Just what the doctor ordered after a great dinner. We passed the joint around and thanked Gigi for inviting us all over. Don't mention it, she responded, you're more than welcome. We'll have to do it again soon. Wouldn't miss this view for the world, it is super cool, Sandy said. We got high, and then, went back inside. Soon after, Mona and Maria returned from the kitchen. Maria said it was past her bedtime and was very pleased to have met us. Pleased to meet you too, your cooking is awesome, good night, I said. Jeff, Sandy and I, gave her a group hug and said goodnight. As Maria headed for bed we turned and thanked Mona for a great night and dinner. Before I go to bed I will give you a personal tour of our house, she said. As Mona took us upstairs, and showed us around, she invited us to spend the night. You've all had way too much to drink and drive, so please, stay the night. These two guest bedrooms have already been prepared for you by Maria. I won't take no for an answer. We promptly accepted her offer. You're so kind, how could we refuse an offer like that, I said. We older folks have to go to bed early, but you kids enjoy your drinks and I'll see you all in the morning for breakfast, good night, Mona said. Sandy, Jeff, Gigi and I went back downstairs for some more dancing and drinks. Jeff and I shared time with each of the girls, it was sweet. We stepped back outside for a joint and all decided it was time for bed. Gigi smiled and led me by the hand back indoors and up the stairs. Jeff and Sandy were following close behind.

Gigi lead us down the long hallway and stopped at the first bedroom on the left. Goodnight, Sandy and Jeff, this will be your bedroom, enjoy. I smiled at Jeff and continued to be pulled by the hand toward the next door, there were several more. Gigi skipped the next door and quietly opened the following one. As we approached the foot of the king size bed, we stopped, embraced, and kissed passionately. As I removed her robe I could see some very pretty bikini panties, which surprised me, simply because she had not been wearing any the entire night. I quickly removed my robe. As we climbed onto the bed and under the covers on the left side, all the way on the right side of the large bed, was a rather large lump. My complete focus was entirely on Gigi's beautiful body, and I didn't pay it much mind. We just cuddled and kissed for a very long time. I thought, this is it, the moment I've been waiting for so long. I couldn't wait any longer and moved in for the kill. I ever so slowly rolled on top of her and placed my erect penis between her legs, which I slowly opened. Mind you, she's still wearing the bikini panties. When I reached for the panties, she grabbed my hands, and said, slow down, I've got something I need to tell you. I prepared for the worst. It was quite a surprise to me, and couldn't have come at a worse time, she said. What is it, I asked? I need you to promise me you'll be patient and wait for the right time for us to make love, please, Gigi begged. I promise, now what is it? It started. What started? It's that time of the month, it just happened about thirty minutes ago, the last time I went to the bathroom. What, I said. You know my menstrual period. I apologize, I know you're disappointed, but I'll make it up to you next time, Gigi said. Now if you don't mind, let's just get some sleep. She rolled over onto her side facing the wall. I kissed her and reassuringly said I totally understand that it will have to wait and you are definitely worth every day I wait. I snuggled up to her backside and held her in my arms tightly, goodnight. Gigi sighed and gently moaned, as if to say she was happy I understood and was very glad I had hugged her tight, like I really cared, and I did. I knew she was worth waiting for. I really liked her a lot. Gigi quickly fell asleep, not I, I was fully erect and wasn't the least bit sleepy, I was horny.

As I lay on my back staring at the ceiling wondering what might have been, I saw for the first time, from a different angle, that the lump had a very nice and very familiar shape. I was so horny that even the larger than life silhouette on the wall, looked enticing. I wasn't sure who it was, but she was on her side with her back to me, just the way Gigi was laying. I slowly slid a little closer as I carefully lifted the sheet to get my first glimpse. Wow she was hot, wearing only a very short teddy, I was shocked, Mona, Gigi's mom, gulp! I was in a trance like state. I had to get a closer look. I lifted the sheet and could see that she was not wearing anything underneath the teddy, oh my, I gulped again. Without a sound, I even sort of held my breath. I turned onto my side and withered in closer so that I was side by side, ever so close. Mona appeared to be dead asleep. Without hesitating or thinking, I carefully positioned myself. Without touching or using my hands, I started visual guidance, of my erect manhood toward my goal. She was positioned just right, sort of curled up, knees up high, with her bottom sticking out towards me. With just the right position I could penetrate her vagina, I calculated. The built up sexual anticipation was something so special, you could only imagine. I got so caught up, it was like a dream like state of mind, crazy. Dare I do this, I thought for a moment, as I continued my course. Surely she was awake and eagerly awaiting my touch, or is she really such a sound sleeper, I wondered. In any case Mona did not move at all, motionless, completely still. I was breathing very hard with no turning back, I was ever so close. It was a precise and perfect placement. I felt moisture and began my slow, ever so slow, penetration. At no point had any part of my body touched her, not one finger. The only contact was penis to the inside of her vagina. First just the head, it felt so good, I didn't want to move. Motionless and without any resistance, quite the opposite, she seemed to be sucking my erection in further and further ever so slowly, it was like a dream. I couldn't believe this was happening. Before long I was 100% totally inside her. Mind you, I'm not small by any means. One of my nicknames in high school was "the cucumber". I sort of just laid there and let her vagina do all the work. No pumping or touching, still just the penetration. Surely she's awake. She still had not made a sound or moved a muscle, couldn't even hear her breath. Either I'm Houdini or she's the best actress in the world, deserving of an Oscar. I was in disbelief, and could not even imagine what was to happen next. At this particular instance the built up sensations began to remind me of my experience with Sandy, not so long ago. I began to climax ever so long and hard. I didn't for one second even consider doing what I had done most of my young life, pull out and come. This was just that good. I continued to come and come and come again. I had never experienced multiple orgasms. I had heard about women doing it, so that's what it feels like, oh my, oh my, I thought, as I continued to climax, over and over, continuously. They stopped, my orgasms that is, but neither one of us moved. It was as if we were trying to fool each other into thinking the other didn't know what was going on, it was a fantastic feeling, indescribably delicious. And I think we both knew it. I didn't dare pull out, it still felt so good. Besides, I might break her concentration, you know, wake her, yea. We just laid there for a few minutes. I was very surprised that I was still hard. Again, I didn't dare pull out. It could ruin everything. You might not believe me, but it all started again, round two, ditto the first, I need not repeat myself, just the same, it was unimaginably just as good. Mona never moved or let on like anything had happened, and we fell asleep. I don't recall ever pulling out.

In the morning I was the first to awake and take a quick shower. Upon exiting the bathroom fully dressed, Gigi was up and kissed me good morning. It was strange. She must have slept through everything. Mona was still motionless and had not even changed positions, weird. Could this have really happened? Maria should be cooking breakfast, I'll take a quick shower and meet you downstairs, she said. I kissed her, and headed for the door. I'm good with that, I figured.

Walking down the hallway past a couple of doors, I simply guessed which one to open because I couldn't remember for sure, the bedroom Sandy and Jeff were in, it took two tries. Quietly opening the door I could see, to no surprise, they were still asleep. As usual, Sandy was exposed and of course I stared at her beautiful body for a few moments. I tip toed quietly so not to wake Jeff, and put my hand on Sandy's shoulder, and shook her ever so gently. She awoke easily, and gave me a great big smile. She grabbed my hand and placed it on her crotch. She was such a tease, I loved that about her. I whispered they should come down to breakfast soon, and that we will expect them in about thirty minutes, please. The main reason I even woke her was that in the back of my mind, my conscience was bothering me, I actually felt very guilty. Had I gone too far last night? I wasn't sure, but for some reason I felt like I wanted to go back to the Holiday Inn Hotel as soon as possible. Maria greeted me with a morning hug and a kiss on the cheek. Everyone will be down in about thirty minutes, I announced. Sit, let's talk, she said. Did you sleep well? Sure did, after that wonderful dinner I fell right to sleep, I lied. Oh that's nice. How about you? I asked. Muy bien, Gracias a Dios, Maria said. Soon, Gigi came in and asked me to help her set the table. Jeff and Sandy came down a few minutes later and joined us for a wonderful meal. Jeff mentioned a 1:00p.m. Deep Sea fishing boat outing at the hotel that he had signed us up for, and that we should leave pretty soon. I felt a sigh of relief, not having to be the one to mention we needed to leave. The sooner the better, I thought. Feeling very guilty and the need to get away, I couldn't have agreed sooner. That sounds like fun, Gigi said, I have to go work. We said our goodbye's, thanks, hugs and kisses and prepared to leave. On the way out, I asked Gigi to meet us at the Salsa Club later that night. I thought that would be an appropriate exit line. She responded with a quick yes, I mean maybe, sure I'll try. We looked around for Jeff's car keys and as soon as we found them, we left for our hotel, whew. I was so glad that I didn't have to face Mona and Gigi. I wasn't quite sure what to expect. Mona never came down, thank God.

That afternoon I experienced deep sea fishing for the first time in my life, it was very exciting. The boat seems so small out in the open sea, it's really a little scary. Jeff had taken Sandy out several times in the Florida area, and they were right at home with the situation. We all caught fish, and were all very happy with the way the afternoon trip had turned out. I caught a rather large swordfish and everyone was quite impressed. The crew caught an eye full of Sandy, and were all very attentive to our needs, especially hers.

Upon returning to the hotel we all showered and took a long nap. When I awoke I was very surprised to see that Sandy and Jeff were already dressing for dinner. Hurry up, get dressed we're starving, Sandy said. After dinner we'll go to the Salsa club and meet Gigi, I hope Mona's with her, Jeff mentions. I was somehow feeling like maybe I wanted to skip that and go to the Rock club instead. I had heard so much about it. Honestly, I was a little hesitant about seeing Gigi. Well I guess there's no getting around facing the consequences with Gigi, let's see what happens, be brave, I thought.

Later that night at the club, Jeff and I danced with Sandy. Gigi was nowhere in sight. I also met some other nice girls that were from New York, Jersey actually. They were sweet, we hit it off for a while and they joined us at our table for some drinks. I was dying to leave the Salsa Club and mentioned the Rock club. Everyone seemed interested so we headed towards the door. On the way out we crossed paths with Gigi and Mona. I was startled, in shock. Gigi stopped and said I see you've met some new friends. By the way, my mom didn't like what you did last night. Oh yea, which time, the first or the second, I responded rather quickly. My come back was so strong it caught them off guard and left them both speechless. Gigi just looked at her mother like she was missing something, as they continued walking. Mona gave me this look as I gazed into her eyes knowing she had enjoyed every minute of the sexual encounter, it was so obvious. We left the club and I knew it was all over between Gigi and me. Maybe it's for the best, I thought. She was expecting more than I had to offer. And as for

Mona, it was well worth it, one, if not the best sexual experience I'd ever had. My new friends, two sisters, Sandy, Jeff and I, just continued our stride and walked out the front door of the bar. I'll explain later, I said to Jeff and Sandy. The others were oblivious to the conversation at hand. We headed down the hall and to the elevator. Why haven't we been to the Rock club? Sandy asked. I just found out about it from a sign in the lobby, yesterday, I said.

Chapter Eight

Rock And Roll

Exiting the elevator, we proceeded down the hallway. The conversation turned into introductions. We hadn't really even introduced ourselves to the sisters, and didn't even know their names. It turns out the sisters were twins, Lee and Dee. They really didn't look like twins. Dee was tall, thin and super beautiful, with a slender physique. On the other hand, Dee was built like a brick house, stacked to the max. Both had blonde hair and blue eyes, they were both hot. After stopping for a brief moment to finish introductory formalities, I continued my fast pace toward the next club, with Lee and Dee in tow. I was sort of pulling them along leading the way not letting go of either one's hand. It was as if I needed them for my escape from Gigi. In the back of my mind I was still thinking about, well honestly, mostly Mona, but Gigi too. I glanced back at Jeff and Sandy, they were all smiles, and following closely. I could tell they were enjoying every minute of the fast pace and sexual tension. Whatever it was, I was on a roll. Again meeting girls was a piece of cake in Acapulco. Love is in the air, you could cut it with a knife.

The club staff at the door smiled at us like they were expecting us. I continued quickly without any hesitation passing the reception and counter area, with my entourage of beautiful people. I always carried myself in this manner, it gets you places. The place was packed. We were still moving swiftly through the crowded aisle; the live rockers were playing a Beatle's tune, "Let It Be". I made eye contact with the singer, a young kid. He stared back, right into my eyes. The melody and the beat were right on, but the vocals, didn't quite match the quality of the music. The kid's timing was spot on, but he had a heavy Mexican accent, and seemed to be improvising on some of the lyrics. He obviously didn't know all the words. He had this look on his face and it was like I was reading his mind. There was a small round table right up front. I stopped long enough to claim our spot, as everyone sat, except for me. I was feeling it. This kid wants me to join them. Without hesitation or missing a stride, I continued, toward the stage. He smiled with approval as his arm reached out with the microphone in hand. Two small steps up, it happened so naturally, almost like it was planned.

I'd been an accompanist all of my young musical life and played lots of guitar, harmony, and backup vocals. I'm no lead singer, but I was on a roll, and I felt very confident in the moment. I certainly knew all the words to lots of Beatle songs, the stuff we play on acoustics back home. We didn't miss a beat, and our table let out a huge roar. I thought I did alright, especially when the drummer asked me to do another song. Do you know our next song to close out our set, "Don't Let Me Down"? Sure, I'd love to sing one more, thanks, I quickly accepted. The crowd reacted very positively as we closed out the set. Break time amigo. Where are you from? San Antonio, Texas, I said. We're all from the capital, Mexico City. Wow, that's a big city I hear. Lencho the drummer mentioned that they were just learning English, but that they played mostly Beatles, Rolling Stones, and sixties rock and roll cover songs they picked up on the radio. That's so cool, I said. It was very early seventies and people in Mexico were just starting to really break into the whole rock thing, the British invasion, that sort of thing. Just like the rest of us, only newer to them. If you could speak English you were very hip to them. And if you could sing, wow. They played it up like I was really good, you know, some sort of star. I laughed, and assured them I wasn't. I'm just like you guys, just breaking out, I said. All this conversation is in Spanish. Meet us backstage in a few, bring your friends. I will, thank you, see you in a few.

Returning to our table, everyone said I did well, and they all gave me a round of applause. I suggested we all dance to the music of the DJ. This is a great club, everyone agreed. All of us danced a few fast songs together and had a couple of drinks. In our conversation I mentioned the group had asked if we would like to join them back stage. Lee and Dee declined and said it was time to meet their parents back in their room. Nice to have met you, maybe we'll see you tomorrow. And they quickly left. Jeff and Sandy declined. You're on your own. We're sleepy and tired, good night. Jeff had already signed the tab for all the drinks, adios amigo.

As I walked through the club on my way backstage, everyone smiled and greeted me. Some younger kids complimented me on my singing. I was in a groovy situation. The drummer, Lencho, welcomed me and introduced me to his girlfriend Alma. We're on our way to the balcony just outside, why don't you join us, there's someone dying to meet you. Once outside, we joined the rest of the band. Everyone was passing around a few joints. This is my cousin from Monterrey, Carmen, Alma says. I've got family, there. I've been there many times. It's a two hour drive to my mom's hometown from there, Monclova, I said.

I've been there many times. Where are you from? Carmen asked. San Antonio, Texas, born and raised, I answer. Well I've heard it is cool, but I've never been, Alma replies. You'll have to come and visit the Alamo and the River Walk. I promise to give you a grand tour. You look and sound a lot like George Harrison, Carmen comments. I'll take that as a huge compliment, that's nice of you to say. I'm flattered. George Harrison is my Idol and mentor. She hugs me and gives me a kiss on the cheek. The chemistry was there.

Once back inside the conversation turned to music. Some of the other members of the band began to quiz me, musically. I love music, it's my life. I live and breathe music. My father was a musician. He was my mentor and inspiration. He played and toured the nation, before settling down and marrying my mom, I went on. He taught me how to play my first instrument, his saxophone. Then I tried the drums, which he threw out the back door of his house. Next I picked up the guitar, which he didn't mind. All the while, Carmen is standing next to me hanging onto my every word. That gave me even more room to talk. With her support and feeling comfortable with the whole group, I was asked to play a song on an acoustic guitar which was propped up in the corner. I quickly accepted. I tuned the classical instrument to my liking. I decided I would dedicate this song to you all for accepting me into your circle of friends and group, I stated. This is something I wrote just recently, I said. Here goes.

"AMIGO"

No matter who you are

Or where you're from

You're my amigo

Hi or low

Or up above

Or down below

You're my amigo

Something new

I'm never blue

Something old

We're always gold

You're my amigo

Some may say

We're not the same

But who's to say

We'll never change

You're my amigo

Time will tell

The power of friends

Good till the end

You're my amigo

That was really nice, is that your own melody and writing? Lencho, asked. You could hear the sound of some applause from the rest of the room. One of my favorites, just for you amigo, I replied. Will you play another song? That was cool. Sure, with pleasure. Mostly I play covers but here goes another original.

"Stay High"

Through my life I've realized

How things used to be

Time has changed my beliefs

Being high, what a relief

When you've realized what life is all about

You regret many past times

But don't fret-you couldn't help it

You didn't know any better

Being high, what a relief

Trying to keep up with times

Specially to keep up with my jive

Dreams, Dreams, Beautiful Dreams,

Don't let them just flow through your mind

Cause your veins, and your brains can't take it-

Being high, what a relief

Get your shit together

Cause later just gets you down

Don't waste precious time

Just keep on trucking and-

Getting down, getting down, getting down

Dreams, Dreams, Beautiful Dreams

Being high, what a relief

Wow, that's heavy shit man. Do you know any Beatles? Sure, so I played "Lucy in the Sky" and John Lennon's, "Imagine", they were impressed. I put the guitar down and grabbed Carmen's hand, and headed back outside to the balcony. I definitely needed some air. We smoked another joint, and talked. I asked Carmen if she would go for a walk on the moon-lit beach, she quickly accepted. I thanked the group and was invited to meet them in the lobby at 6:00pm the next day for a gig at some high school gym. I'll be there 6:00pm sharp, thanks. Carmen grabbed her purse and we said goodnight to Lencho and Alma. You have our blessing, have a good time, they laughed. After a stroll on the sandy beaches of Acapulco, I made my move with Carmen. We kissed and I convinced her to join me for a swim. I slowly undressed her. She was wearing matching bra and panties, very sexy. I always wear bikini men's underwear. Now properly attired, we entered the warm ocean. The natural movement of the waves pressed our bodies so close. Between the under tow current and the movement of the waves, I was surely ready to try and enter her. I made the decision to slow it down a notch, and be more patient, she was definitely worth it. We picked up our clothes and shoes and walked down the beach to air dry. As we walked I told her about the suite at the Holiday Inn, and about my roommates. We could shower, I suggested. I'll call room service, what do you say. I'm starving, I said. Carmen quickly accepted my invitation.

Once in the room, I called and ordered up burgers and fries. Jeff and Sandy were passed out in a coma. I asked Carmen to shower first and handed her a white terry cloth hotel robe. She took it and entered the bathroom. I removed my wet underwear and put on a robe. Sandy looked so good, I couldn't help watch her. As usual she was fully exposed. I turned on the T.V. and cleared the table. I faced the T.V. and pretended to watch the tube. But I was actually watching Sandy's show, it's much better than anything on the air. When Carmen came out she was amused by the show, both the television and Sandy's. She smiled and sat down. Just sign for the food, if it comes, I said. She glanced at me then looked at Sandy and smiled, ok, as I headed for the shower. I couldn't help but thank my lucky stars, love is in the air. You have to experience it to believe it, "Love is definitely in the air in Acapulco".

My timing was perfect, as I exited the bathroom, in my robe, there was a knock on the door. I'll get that Carmen, I'm sure it's room service. The waiter rolled in the service cart and held out his hand. I shook it jokingly and quickly tipped him with the bill in my other hand. He smiled at me and said, muchas gracias senor, buenas noches. Si, gracias a usted, I said. I guided the cart the rest of the way across the room and right in front of the couch that Carmen was sitting on. Your dinner is served miss. Of course you know our conversation is always and completely in Spanish, I presume you know I'm telling this story in English. Later I will do the story in all Spanish, maybe French, Japanese, I'm fiddling again. As I uncovered the plates, you could see that the cheese burgers were made Mexican style with a slice of ham and topped with an avocado wedge, hmmm, and lots of homemade French fries on the side. We enjoyed the rather large meal while watching some sort of late night game show that was on T.V. Mexican stations really show some sexy women, especially late night. It was great for establishing the mood I was trying to set for my next move on Carmen. I rolled an after dinner joint and asked Carmen to join me for a tour around the pool and bar area just outside our sliding glass doors. Your room is really nice. She was impressed with the whole setup, seeing how we were the only room literally attached to the pool side. We found a couple of patio chairs in a private corner and I lit the joint. While we smoked and talked, I noticed she wasn't wearing anything underneath her robe. The pool looked so inviting I had to offer her a late night dip. I promise Sandy won't mind if you wear one of her many bikinis, I mentioned. To my surprise she offered up a better suggestion. I'll just put my matching bra and panties back on, she said. Great idea, let's do it. They really do look like any other swim suit I assured her. We changed and went for a swim like no other. We soon were literally attached. I went in for the kill, she offered little resistance. There's something about making love in the water, it feels very different. The chance someone is watching, or maybe getting caught in the act, just adds to the excitement. As I held her tight and looked deep into her eyes I let her know right then and there that I wanted her to spend the night with me and continue our love making in a bed. This is no quickie, I said. I really like you a lot and want you all night. She didn't need say a word. The look on her face was enough to let me know that the feeling was mutual. She just stared at me with this look of satisfaction on her face, and I could tell it was for real. We soon reached a wonderful climax. Well I'm sure I did, pulling out just to be safe. We adjusted our clothing and exited the pool. My roommates were still motionless as we reentered the suite. I removed her wet bra and panties and guided her towards the bed. We were locked in a very deep embrace as I kissed her wonderful mouth. We sort of just tilted towards the bed and gravity took over as we fell perfectly together without separating our bodies. Carmen climbed on top and I totally let her do her thing. She rode me like a horse and would next climb down my body and place my soaked member in her mouth, without ever touching it. She would suck fast and furiously. Then climb back up by placing her hands on my legs, then my side, and last my shoulders. It was very sensual, this climbing thing, sort of like some kind of ritual she had made up, whatever it was I loved it. She repeated this sequence over and over, she moved very fast, which made it so exciting. I never wanted it to end. It was different, it was new to me. This wonderful sex act was another great learning experience. Each time she placed my wet shaft in her mouth, freshly soaked from her vagina the sensation was wild. If you close your eyes and lay back, it seems like your screwing one girl and getting a blow job from another when the rhythm gets fast enough, it's amazing. I held out as long as I could then was erupting like a volcano. She lapped it all up and swallowed it like she really enjoyed it. You have a very nice taste, not at all salty like most men, Carmen blurted out, between swallows. It was my turn. She was most deserving, as I dove down between her legs head first. She was soaking wet. Carmen you have this wonderful and sexy taste too, I said. I douched earlier with strawberry delight, you like? I continued without missing a lap. It really was very natural. I would have never guessed douching had anything to do with the taste. I could have continued a lot longer but she grabbed my head and pulled me in very hard and held me pressed tightly against her vagina. I was motionless except for my tongue, of course. She shuttered and squeezed my head with her legs as she obviously climaxed several times. We showered together and jumped back in the queen sized bed as we finally fell asleep in one tight and final embrace.

I was dreaming when I awoke. The sun shining through the open drapes not only had a heavenly rainbow of colors it brought a ray of light so inspirational I grabbed a pen and paper and wrote several lines.

"Dreams Do Come True"

Follow me to the top

When I think back

I always thought

You'd follow me to the top

Take hold of my hand

I've got just what you need

There'll be no questions asked

I can promise you that

There'll be no luggage to pack

I can assure you that

There'll be no regrets

Take hold of my hand

There'll be no ticket for that

Dreams do come true

I can promise you that

Take hold of my hand

Fly with me

I'll hold you tight

Through the Galaxy

We might never come back

I've got just what you need

I can promise you that

Dreams do come true

I can assure you that

Fly with me

I'll hold you tight

When I think back

When I think back

Dreams do come true, Dreams do come true

Everyone else was still sleeping, when I heard a faint tap or slight knock at the door. Peering through the peep hole I could see it was room service. As I opened the door to a Buenos Dias, room service greeting, the cart rolled in. On top a large tray of whole fresh strawberries. Next to them, a fondue type pot of melted dark chocolate on a flame and some long spear like forks to use to dip the fruit. Underneath were plates, flute glasses and a bottle of champagne on ice. The attendant handed me a note. I in turn went in search of a dollar bill or some pesos for the gratuity. On the night stand next to Jeff were two or three small bills, I borrowed the five American, and handed it to the gentleman. Gracias amigo, have a nice day. A note read: We're guessing you two are still together, so enjoy, thanks for singing with us. See you tonight, the Band.

I got back in bed and gave Carmen a slight hug as to wake her peacefully. Surprise, look what your sister Alma and Lencho and the band went out of their way to do for us this morning, they're so cool. This is nothing, they're always surprising me, she said. They do stuff like this all the time. They're very romantic like that, always meaning to, well, sort of trying to, hook me up with mister right, if you get my drift, they mean well. Well we could all use more of that kind of thoughtfulness and kindness, I know I never get that kind of attention, you're very fortunate to have friends and family like that. What a sweet gesture, I said. Now let's enjoy like the note says. After finishing the champagne and some of the strawberries, we dressed for breakfast and headed downstairs. Afterwards I walked her to her room and kissed her goodbye. I'll see you at 6:00pm, I said, you know for the show. Right and don't be late, she said jokingly. I wouldn't miss it for the world, I assured her, later.

About a quarter to six I headed to the lobby only to be surprised by a small crowd that had gathered in the hotel lobby. Turns out "La Tribu" had just released their third album and were having a meet and greet in the lobby. Carmen greeted me with a kiss, as everyone else smiled and continued with what they were doing, signing albums and band photos for the giveaway. Afterwards I was asked to join Lencho for a photo shoot. Everyone thought we looked like brothers. I'm guessing the long straight black hair had a lot to do with that. Anyway, I guess I fit right in looking like one of the crew or band members. A little after six most of the guys headed out the front door of the hotel and we were to follow once Lencho wrapped up the meet and greet, from what I had gathered, or had heard, made out, you know what I mean. Alma, Lencho, Carmen and I headed out the front door as a rather large bus pulled up. How do you like it? Wow, is that the band's bus, I asked, in my amazement. We've been quite fortunate these last several years, Lencho says, all aboard for our next gig. Sleeps eight you know, you could join us on the road if you like. We leave for Cancun tomorrow. What a great offer you're too kind, but I'm due back in San Antonio soon, back to school. College means a lot to my dad and mom, besides I'm already registered for the spring semester, they'd kill me, I couldn't. It's already been paid for. Oh you know what I mean. We understand, just asking mostly for Carmen's sake, she's always so lonely. Funny, Carmen adds, yea right.

Well anyway what's tonight's gig all about? I ask. It's a high school dance, three forty five minute sets, then we're back on the road to Cancun, you dig. Lots of young kids, you'll have to sing a few songs to earn your keep. I can do that. This will be great experience for you with such a young crowd, it'll be a piece of cake, Lencho promises. We board the bus and head to the school. Show Z-Bird the R.V. Give him the grand tour of the bus. Z-Bird is, and always has been my code name, or stage name. Once back in our seats next to Lencho and Alma, Lencho crosses his legs, twists the black heel of his Beatle boots to reveal a secret little compartment, his stash. Pulling out a small plastic zip lock bag containing several orange tabs, or tablet form pills, if you will. You like Acid, L.S.D., he asks? This is Orange Sunshine, here take one. Alma, Carmen, Lencho and I, all take a tab. First time for me, I'm a little nervous, what's it like? Sit back and enjoy, you're in for the ride of your life. Ok, thanks, I guess. Carmen just smiled. Here's a copy of our song list for tonight. Look it over on the way to the gym. Let me know which two or three songs you feel comfortable singing with us. Let's just say I'll do some of the Beatle songs, at least I'm sure I know the words.

Upon arriving, via backstage, we were offered drinks and a few munchies on a folding table. Twenty five minutes till show time, Lencho announced. Some of the band remained with the bus, and unloaded guitars, but the roadies handled the rest of the equipment. I'm headed to the Men's Room. I want you to help with sound check in ten minutes, please, Lencho demands.

The Acid kicked in and I was tripping pretty hard. The gig went on without a hitch. I was greeted and by the sounds of the applause, did quite well during the third and final set. I truly enjoyed it. We were back on the bus in no time. Carmen and I sit in the middle section of the bus and start making out like there's no tomorrow. Next thing you know the bus is on this dark highway, headed to who knows where. I'm very concerned about the direction we're traveling in, something just doesn't feel right. Every band member and every person on the bus is totally smashed, and everyone is laughing uncontrollably, including me. Don't worry it's the Acid, Carmen says, as she gets up and says, I'll be right back, sit tight. Somehow I was under the impression no one was listening to me at all. There's been some sort of confusion. I need to be dropped off at the Holiday Inn. It was obvious no one had told the bus driver. Everyone was in their own little world, no worries. Again I say I need to be dropped back at the hotel. Everyone ignores me. I began to realize that the situation was out of control. Even

Lencho looked at me, finally, like the situation was not in his hands. So someone else is pulling the strings. Who could it be? I got out of my seat and headed back through the aisle and towards the back of the bus/R.V. Wow, at that moment I felt like I was where everyone else was, totally smashed and rather confused. I was definitely seeing color trails and traces of moving objects, very blurry and varied color schemes. So this is what normally repressed psychic elements exposed by the drugs, (L.S.D.) are causing in everyone's minds, including me. I was only glad I had not taken the second tab everyone else had taken. I had been very smart by turning it down, because I could barely maintain as it was. Now I was beginning to understand why everyone seemed so flipped out, they were. Now it began to make sense. No one really wanted me to come against my will, it just sort of happened. I was certainly paranoid enough to imagine the worst plot against me. For some reason rather than head towards the bus driver, I continued towards the rear. Still thinking about Carmen, I guess. I was beginning to sense there was something about Carmen, Carmen, I said loudly. No response. Suddenly I heard a familiar voice, it was her, without hesitating, using both arms, I split open a rather large partition like curtain. Some manager type older man in a pin stripped suit was embracing Carmen as she laughed at the sight of me opening the curtain to one of the private sleeping areas. I handled it well, just wanted to say goodbye, I'm getting off the bus at the next stop, later. I turned quickly without waiting for any reply and headed quickly up the aisle towards the bus driver.

The driver, a kind senior citizen dressed in dark blue overalls wearing a cap informed me that they always head for the next location when that city's dates are all done. And that we were, he assured me. The driver sort of chuckled and said it wasn't the first time and it wouldn't be the last to have to pull over and let someone out. They won't allow me to turn around ever, time is of the essence, he said, or else I would, sorry. You see, "La Tribu" has a wedding in Cancun tomorrow afternoon. So you see we're on a tight schedule. There's a small town coming up, we're only twenty seven miles out of Acapulco. There is a small bus station on this highway or you could catch one of many vans that head out every hour on the hour from that point back to town, that's the best I can do, sorry. Sounds good, no problem, Amigo. I let the kind man know that I understood it wasn't his fault and told him I'd be right back. To my surprise, Lencho and Alma weren't in their seats. It was obvious they had gone to bed, and I wasn't about to go looking for them for fear of what I might encounter on that bus. I went back and decided to get off the bus without any goodbyes. So I asked the driver for a piece of paper and pen. He pointed to a small black brief case and said help yourself young man.

I was in a creative state of mind which surprised me with all that was going on so quickly, I was tripping on acid for Heaven's sake. So I quickly took the front row seat and began writing a few lines. The lines turned into verses, and I wasn't sure why, but, I just kept on writing.

"Time Traveler"

Once there was a way

Time to throw away

I was all you had

And I thought I was bad

Time is all we had

Time to throw away

Time is of no objection

After a reflection

An image of you in a bay

Time is all we had

Time just wasting away

But what do you expect?

From an LSD trip

Time to spare

Rare but spare times

Time is all we had

After all we've eaten together

Let's at least get along, lady

Boom just like that, it was over. My mind was back to how in the world I would get back to Acapulco and the hotel where more problems awaited my arrival. I never gave any of my writings much thought, they kind of just flow through me, as if they aren't really even mine. I'm never really happy with them but I don't try and change them. I believe that the original thought must be worth preserving and just let them be, what is meant to be. I don't even care if they are really well written, rhyme or any good, they're original. I've really never shared them with anyone till now. I was nineteen, what the hell.

We pulled up along the bus station and I quickly hopped out. Muchas gracias Amigo, I said to the bus driver. Adios, buena suerte, goodbye and good luck, he replied. As I walked into the terminal I reached for my wallet. How much money do I have anyway? I knew it wasn't much. I walked up to the ticket counter and was informed the next bus to Acapulco was scheduled to depart the station at 2:45a.m. I was afraid to ask my next question, how much for the ticket? Sixty five pesos, she said. How much in U.S. currency, American, and do you accept dollars? Sure do. It is five dollars and twenty five cent American, sir, she replied. I was in luck. I had about six dollars and seventy five cents. I bought my ticket, and asked for a pen and paper, she obliged. It was about one thirty in the morning and with an hour to kill and still tripping I figured in my state of mind I'd be better off sitting still and using my mind to maybe write another couple of verses. Still feeling a little down about the way things turned out with Carmen I felt the need to write what I was feeling.

"What A Cad"

Life lived through dreams

As always it seems

Is no means of survival

Ever since your arrival

Time to waste with you

Will always make me blue

Cause you're so true

And I'm so blue

Blues Bag Lady don't be lazy

Lazy Lady find yourself another cad

Cause I've been had too long

Being had, what a drag

Out of it, cause your hip

What a trip couldn't help it. Cause I'm really down

I don't know, is this writing anything worth saving? I ask myself, I guess so. I always did, save them, that is. To this day I still have these writings. I put away the pen and paper and thought I might have to try and find something to eat, maybe that will help bring me down off this mind trip. Boy was I ready. Just outside the terminal was a vendor's cart with some greasy street tacos. Beef, I was told. Can I get a soda and some tacos for this last dollar bill? Please! The tacos were very small corn tortillas filled with chopped beef, smothered in onions and topped with lots of cilantro. Here you go, just add your own salsa, the vendor said, as he took the dollar bill. Quite tasty amigo, they were very delicious. I finished my meal and headed back inside to the men's room. To my amazement the intercom announcement was my bus number and time to hop on board to Acapulco. Looking at my watch I noticed it was right on time, something I hadn't anticipated, a Mexican bus on time, strange. I boarded the bus, found a seat near the driver for some conversation and settled in for the forty-five minute ride. I was getting sleepy, which was a good sign. I remember thinking. Rock and roll isn't all that it's cracked up to be, then, I dozed off.

Chapter Nine

Adios

Upon arrival back in Acapulco, I found myself in a strange part of town. Downtown Acapulco, somewhere I had never been. It was not like the popular tourist area by the bay. I had gotten use to the ease of getting around by looking up at the hotels and using them to know where I was. I noticed what appeared to be a lot of locals hanging out at the cab stand and quickly headed toward them figuring I could get some directions from someone, maybe a cab driver. I knew I would have to walk being completely out of cash. I was hoping it wasn't going to be too far. A young cab driver standing by his beat up car was very helpful and walked me around the corner of the building where you could actually see some of the hotels, and the direction in which I needed to start walking. Thanks, I said, as I was walked towards the beautiful sight of those huge hotels. They looked very close. Looks can be deceiving, I quickly realized they weren't. As I walked and walked I thanked my lucky stars I was back in Acapulco and I had this really bad feeling in my stomach, (gut), that it was really time to start heading back to San Antonio and get ready to go back to school. I was hoping to find Sandy and Jeff in our hotel room and maybe convince them it was time to head back. The walk was long, about forty minutes. Thirsty and hot, I quietly opened the door to our room. They were passed out. I found something to drink took a quick shower and got in my bed.

In the morning, I was the last to awake, which was very unlike me. Considering the acid trip I had just taken, the hassle and the walk back, I slept like a baby. Believe it or not, Jeff and Sandy would have no part of leaving. They laughed and laughed. What the hell is wrong with you boy, enjoy. I'm paying for everything, relax, you still have a few more days before you need to be home.

The next few days Sandy and Jeff seemed to be hibernating again and hardly ever left the room. I was on my own, wandering around the hotel signing for food and drinks. The days passed quickly and I met lots of new people daily. One afternoon, I met a guy who introduced himself to me by the swimming pool bar, John Mills from Dallas, Texas. He was the only person I met from my state. We drank a couple of beers at the bar and spent some time swimming and talking. During our conversation, John mentioned he was dying to smoke a joint but hadn't had any luck finding any. He said he had an ice chest full of beer and would be happy to get it from his room and share it if I could get us a joint. We went for the beer and headed for our room. I knocked first and upon entering the suite we found Jeff and Sandy under the covers saying come on in. They appeared happy to see a new young face. I introduced them and offered them a beer from John's ice chest. There were a few joints already rolled up on the night stand. Sandy sparked one up and handed it to John. As Sandy sat up it was obvious she was topless. About fifteen minutes into our little party, Jeff whispered something into Sandy's ear and she jumped out of bed totally nude and started running around the room with Jeff laughing and chasing her around. Jeff picked up a hair brush and paddled Sandy on the butt a few times as he chased her around. They laughed and thought it was funny and amusing. John seemed to enjoy the show for about a minute, then freaked out and headed for the door. I handed him a joint for the road as he made a quick exit. I never saw that kid again. Jeff was always doing crazy things like that and it was getting old quick. I believe to this day Jeff had multiple personalities, Dr. Jekyll and Mr. Hyde kind of stuff, if you know what I mean. I was getting nervous being around these two people more and more every day, especially as of late. I think I had had enough of them for a lifetime. I was also beginning to wonder about all the expenses we were incurring daily. They must really be mounting up to quite some bill. It just didn't add up anymore, something didn't seem right. This was too good to be true, and you know what they say about that. My instincts were starting to tell me something was definitely wrong with these two. Not having much of a choice in the matter at hand, I put off all the warning signs I was getting, and went back to playing their little game again.

That same evening, Jeff wanted to go to dinner, and then to one of the clubs we hadn't visited yet. What the hell I thought, what else can I do? So I fell right back into the same old trap of trusting Jeff and went right along with his request for me to come along with them. They were both on their best behavior the entire evening and actually seemed to be a loving couple, holding hands and kissing, stuff like that. After a great seafood buffet dinner, dessert included, we headed up the elevator to the top floor of the hotel where we were to find the Blues Club. The drinks were flowing and we were having a grand old time. Sandy asked me to dance. Jeff wasn't much of a dancer, so of course I was glad to fill in for him. The live Blues music was very different but still danceable. Sandy and I would come together fast and hard as we danced. She would press her leg hard between my legs and push her thigh hard on my crotch. She knew exactly what she was doing, getting me very riled up and super horny for her. As we danced I made eye contact with a very pretty young lady. She smiled back at me as we sat down. I watched her very closely as to see where she was sitting. The very next song I made a B-line towards her table, she smiled as I approached. Would you care to dance? I asked. She got up quickly and we went to the center of the dance floor. I introduced myself and she said her name was Marion Wells. My next question, where are you from Marion? I'm from Boulder, Colorado, she whispered in my ear as I pulled her closer as we danced. What about you? She asked. I'm from and live in Texas, San Antonio, Texas. We talked about her hometown, (I'd never been to Colorado) it sounded really neat, lots of snow. We don't really see much snow in San Antonio. After our dance she held my hand and pulled me right along with her to meet her friends. I joined them and bought a round of drinks. We could have danced all night. We danced well together, I was impressed, her being from Boulder and all. Romance was in the air, I just love Acapulco. I held her very close for several slower songs. It was getting late, and she mentioned they would be leaving the club to go to their rooms. As we said our goodbyes, I asked her to join us for lunch the following day. She said she would try and that twelve noon at the main buffet by the pool sounded cool. After Marion left I went back and joined Jeff and Sandy. Sit, time for more dancing and drinks, Sandy said. I was having a good night with the ladies. Besides dancing with Sandy, I danced with several other pretty young women. The whole time in the back of my mind I was stilling thinking about the next day with Marion. Jeff was tired and ready to leave and got up from the table. He mentioned that if we liked, we could stay and dance some more and that he would see us later in the room. Sandy smiled and kissed Jeff on the lips and said, thank you darling, we won't be too late. She grabbed my hand and quickly guided me to the middle of the dance floor again. Turns out Sandy loves the Blues, oh so slow and seductive, she whispers in my ear. After Jeff left we just stayed out on the dance floor song after song. During a very slow song, Sandy mentioned she had been partially awake during my evening in bed with Peggy Johnson, and had watched me make love to her. Things got very heated at that point as she got me very aroused. We sat for one last drink, after I suggested we call it a night. As I gathered my composure, closed our tab, we finally left rather abruptly. In the elevator on the way down, we made out like never before, it was nice. Then, Sandy went down on me, my first experience in an elevator, cool, I moaned. It didn't take me long, as she gobbled my goop, and I quickly zipped it back up just in time for the door to open. Peering out the elevator door, it was clear, no one around our hallway, exit stage left for a clean getaway. Upon entering the suite Jeff was passed out as usual, out like a light. I was seriously tired after all the dancing and hit the sack, Sandy entered the bathroom. I was dozing off when she came out totally nude. What a beautiful sight. Surprisingly she made a mad dash for her own bed. I being exhausted didn't move a muscle, pretending to be asleep.

I awoke early the next day. Just thinking about the lunch date with Marion made me anxious. Will she show? She sure seemed like a very nice girl, probably from a well to do, educated family. I decided to swim some laps in the pool directly outside our room. I'm quite the swimmer, by the age of sixteen I was a lifeguard at our local public pool, San Pedro. In middle school I had been on the swim team and had some impressive times on the fifty yard individual, and two hundred yard relay team. I was surely feeling a bit hung over and decided to go for the full treatment. The most effective way to cure a hangover despite what you might have heard through the years is my special method. It always works, and I guarantee it, you'll be ready to drink a six pack if you follow my instructions, I promise you this has never failed me yet. First you must swim at least ten laps in the pool. Second, jump into the Jacuzzi for fifteen minutes. Next the steam room for about twenty minutes. Drink some water and take a quick cold shower, and repeat everything except the swimming if you like, several times as needed. Depending on the severity of your hangover, there you have it. Happy and cured I guarantee it, ready for your next party. When I was all done, I headed back to the pool and ordered a Corona beer with a lime and some salt on the rim of the glass, Mexican style. Suddenly Sandy came out in her white itsy bitsy bikini, Jeff was following her not far behind. They were both smiling and appeared to be very happy to see me. Turns out Jeff wanted me to escort them down for another turn at water skiing on the Acapulco Bay. That would be my pleasure, let's grab our towels and one of the hotel keys and go to the beach. Jeff acted like a perfect gentleman all morning. That's what always got me into trouble with Jeff, he could be so kind and gentle one minute and next he would act like a total asshole. Sandy pretty much was her same sexy self all the time. We all skied till we were dead tired and Jeff signed off on the bill. Next we hung out on the beach in front of our hotel and had some cocktails. I had thought about meeting with Marion alone, but felt awkward when Jeff suggested we get changed and have some lunch. We'd had such a great morning what could I say. While dressing I mentioned my date and they seemed happy for me. I was somewhat surprised when Marion showed up on time accompanied by her family. As they headed to the buffet line smiling I figured she had already told them about me and our lunch date. Marion came over and joined us as her family served themselves. I introduced her to Jeff and Sandy as we got in line. Everything went well at lunch and the conversation was perfect. Sandy and Marion seemed to hit it off. They were about the same age, I'm guessing. Jeff was well behaved and was the perfect host. Jeff signed off on the lunch and they went up for a nap, accordingly. Marion accepted my invitation for a walk on the beach. We spent the entire afternoon together. After watching the sun set on the beach, I walked her to the elevators. Marion mentioned she was doing stuff with her family that night but would meet me again the next day, same time and place. It's a date, and I kissed her goodbye.

When I got back to the room, they were ready to go out on the town. I showered and while I was dressing mentioned the fact that I had heard a lot about the famous cliff divers at a nearby hotel. Sounds like fun, Jeff answered. Sandy seemed excited about the whole idea. On the way out I asked for directions at the front desk. It was a short drive to the hotel where the performance would take place. We were staying sort of in the middle of the Acapulco Bay area, (the bay is shaped like a horseshoe) this hotel was sort of on the end of the horseshoe like shape of the bay, the high side. As we parked you could see that the view from this vantage point was totally different, much higher. We walked in and were offered dining indoor or outdoor seating. I spoke up and said it was our first time and that we wanted a table up front outside by the cliff divers. The Maitre d' escorted us to the observation deck and totally sat us at the best table available right up in front. Jeff handed the man a gratuity. He smiled and pulled the chair out for Sandy to be seated, really a first class joint, I was impressed. We ordered some drinks and were told the show would start shortly. We ordered dinner and enjoyed the view of the bay. Sandy was flirting as usual playing footsy under the linen laced table with me. Once the diving started it was so exciting. I'd never seen anything like it. Some of the divers were holding flaming torches on the way down to the ocean. The tide came in and out with perfect harmony, timing of the rhythm of the wave was crucial to surviving the dive. Jeff boasted that he thought he could do the dive. Our waiter mentioned that it had only been done a few times by hotel guests and said it's done only during the day, and only after the person signs a disclaimer against the hotel and the property owners, but I wouldn't recommend it, he said. Our divers have been diving for years and it is usually a family tradition handed down from generation to generation. Sandy and I just laughed at the thought of Jeff diving. End of conversation. It was a fabulous dinner and show. Jeff used the American Express Gold Card, paid the bill, and we left. Next we drove up the strip and stopped at a local bar/club. We stayed till they closed the place at around 4 a.m. and we called it a night heading back to our hotel.

The next morning we all slept in. My plans with Marion were a driving force for me to get out of bed and shower. I put on my new Hawaiian shirt and matching swim suit and went out to the pool, bar and buffet area. To my surprise Marion was already swimming in the pool and I hardly recognized her with her hair all wet. She was very cute and had a sexy body. She joined me for lunch and after we headed for the beach. In the bay as we swam, I held her close and kissed her long and hard for the first time. She seemed to enjoy it at first, then, said she wanted to be totally honest with me, and didn't want to lead me on. I can't do this anymore. What, I asked. Lead you on. I haven't been fair to you or my boyfriend back home in Colorado, I'm very sorry. Don't be, it's been a lot of fun, I've really enjoyed your company and being just friends and hanging out is just fine with me. I guess she expected a different reaction from me, as she gave me a big hug and kissed me on the lips. Thanks for understanding you're so cool. Haven't I been the perfect gentleman? I said laughing. Indeed you have, and that's what I like about you the most, she said. It doesn't have to be all about sex you know, I said. We had a great understanding and I continued to see her for the next couple of days.

I hadn't really been paying much attention to a calendar or kept track of the days we had been in Acapulco, but they were going fast. I'm going to guess and I think we'd been in Acapulco for about thirteen days and it was January 6th, 1971. This particular day had started out like many of the other days when Sandy and Jeff were still crashed out and I would head out on my own. Out in front of the hotel was my usual palapa and I quickly claimed it as mine for the time being. The same one as always, the same one I had met Gigi and Mona under, it became my very personal hangout, sort of my bachelor pad, you might say, lucky spot. While swimming on the beach, I met a couple of long haired hippie type guys that said they were from Canada, Montreal. They spoke with heavy accents and seemed to be very worldly and cool, kind of classy, just slightly older than I. I asked them what Canada was like as I offered to share the shade of my Palapa. They were carrying a small ice chest and handed me a beer. This is Ron and I'm David. My name is Tony, and I'm from San Antonio, Texas. They mentioned they had been to Sixth Street in Austin, and were into the music scene there. We're musicians. I told them that I played a little guitar and tried to sing mostly backup. I bought us a round of Margaritas as we continued to talk about music. We finished the beer and drinks and they asked if I wanted to come up to their room and play some guitar. I got up in a flash, sounds like fun, and we headed inside and down the hallway towards the elevators. Once in the room I could smell a familiar aroma as David came out of the bath area holding a smoking pipe, and a guitar. Ron reached under the bed and pulled out a case with another guitar and they started to jam. I smoked some of their pot, it was really good, Acapulco gold, David said. It's the best shit around, I promise you that. We all took turns playing, as they shared their weed and guitars with me. About an hour later I invited them down to the dining room for a late lunch, as a token of my appreciation of their kindness and new friendship. I signed off on the bill and David said, come by our room anytime, as we parted ways. They thanked me for lunch, and I said goodbye.

On the way through the hotel lobby, I was called over to the front desk by an older gentleman in a dark suit. Where is Jeff Anderson? I was asked. He introduced himself as the head of security for the Holiday Inn Hotel. I told him that Jeff was probably with his girlfriend Sandy in our room. Is there anything I can help you with? I need to speak to Mr. Anderson right away concerning his hotel bill. The hotel manager has brought to my attention the fact that Mr. Anderson has gone over the limit on his American Express Card. I need you to let him know I need to speak to him right away. I'm sure there's been some sort of mistake, Jeff is a very wealthy man, I said. Listen son, do you even know who you are associated with. You need to listen to me very carefully. I figured I'd give you fair warning, you being a young Mexican American and all. You might have to thank me later son. If this turns out to be a problem, just you signing off on food and drinks could make you an accomplice if any crimes have been committed. These are serious allegations. You don't want to end up in a Mexican jail. I can assure you that they are terrible accommodations. Not like in the States. I will bring Jeff down to the front desk as soon as I locate him, I promised. Thank you for the inside information and I headed towards the room quick. At no time did he ask my name or who I was, thank God, I'm not sure what I would have said.

When I got back to the room, Jeff and Sandy were loaded as usual, smoking pot and drinking, and by the way the room looked, drugged out on pills. I wasn't sure exactly how to say what I had to say so I just started talking and explaining what had just happened at the front desk. When I told Jeff what was going down he totally freaked out and told Sandy to start packing. He went over to the night stand and grabbed the car keys. Next to their bed and from under the mattress he pulled out a pistol and pointed it at my face and said, you got us into this mess, now you are going to have to get us out of it you little prick. Somehow Jeff blamed me for everything. I froze and didn't dare say one word. I was never so scared in all my life. Pack your shit, we're getting out of here now, Jeff screamed. Judging from Jeff's reaction, I knew we were in big trouble. Sandy was throwing bags of their stuff towards the front door. Jeff threw the car keys in my direction as they hit the wall hard. He ordered me to gather some of the bags and start making some trips down the back steps to the parking garage. Without hesitation I grabbed all that I could carry, all the while Jeff was still holding the gun on me. Hurry, we have a lot to load, the suitcases will be waiting for you when you get back. Fortunately for me, our room was on the third floor and pretty close to the emergency exit that leads me right down to the parking garage. It could have been higher up the thirty story hotel and been a much longer and gruesome journey. It took me three trips to finish with their stuff and was exiting the staircase on our floor when I noticed a familiar uniform. It was that of an armed security man now standing guard by the stairs. Obviously he was just getting to his post for the rest of the evening when I slipped right passed him. I turned the corner quickly and was sweating like a pig and nervous as hell. I surely didn't want to be confronted at that moment. I got lucky and made sure he wasn't watching me, and entered our room. All that was left was my small blue suitcase. I told Jeff about the security guard standing by the steps and let him know that I wanted to wait till later with my things. Somehow I had to convince him. Okay let me think, Jeff pondered. We'll definitely wait, all the drugs are in Sandy's suitcase so we are clean. We'll wait till the coast is clear and then make our move in the wee hours of the morning, Yes, that's what we'll do, Jeff mumbled. We'll just relax and watch T.V. As I lay in my bed I must have dozed off.

I awoke and thought I was having a bad dream. Not a chance. It was Jeff giving me a nudge on the shoulder to wake up. It's time, go take a look around the exits for a quick getaway. Everything was still the same. The same guy was by the stairs I had used earlier. I headed for the elevators and down to the lobby. It looked like the hotel was in a code red alert. Every exit was covered by security. They were checking everyone leaving the hotel. I headed to a nearby phone booth near the lobby and pretended to make a call. It appeared that security was stopping anyone carrying luggage and asking them for the hotel checkout receipt and I.D. I wasn't sure what to do but decided to go back to our room and report my findings. On the way up in the elevator I spoke to a room service type employee and asked him what was up with all the security. It's the holidays, this is pretty much the norm, hotel security just trying to keep the walk outs to a minimum. It happens every year during the holidays. We have a lot of people trying to take advantage of the crowds and the confusion that goes with it. Lots of people over do it, you know, spend way too much, and don't want to suffer the consequences by signing for large hotel bills and truly believe they can easily deny them from the comfort of their homes. Can you believe that? No, not really, I said. Unconsciously I passed my third floor and for some unknown reason went up to the seventh floor, which was David and Ron's floor. I was scared and very worried about the whole situation. Maybe I needed some courage, I'm not sure. A diversion of some sort, or maybe I was just stalling. There it was I was so sure, room 707, yea, that's it. I knocked. I was in luck, they were still awake. David opened the door and immediately invited me in. Ron passed me a joint, and David handed me a guitar. I sort of felt better already, and was glad I had come up. Halfway through the first song I stopped playing and told them I was in big trouble. I just about broke down and cried on the couch. They were very supportive and David said not to worry that everything would be alright. Ron looked at David and as he spoke, very surprisingly, David made me an unforgettable offer. I couldn't believe what he had just said, and Ron agreed with a nod. David said he would drive me to Mexico City in the morning, and I could take a Greyhound Bus to San Antonio, Texas from there. I was so embarrassed. That's so cool, but I haven't got the bus fare. I'll drive you and lend you the money, amigo. I accepted his life saving offer. We made plans to meet out in front of the hotel at precisely 9:00a.m. I'll have to stall with Jeff, but that was the earliest David said we could leave for some reason. I felt quite relieved, and immediately began to wonder how I would get away from Jeff and Sandy. I at the least had some help and the beginning of some sort of plan. I began to get very nervous again and decided it was time to get back and face Jeff.

When I got back to the room Jeff was furious, where have you been and what took you so long? I needed to stall for time, I thought to myself. David would not be ready to leave till 9:00 a.m. I figured I'd have to try and convince Jeff to wait till morning to make our move. I began to explain the security situation to them. So ah, the stairs are covered as well as the front and back entrances. Has anyone come to our door asking any questions? I asked. They both answered no at the same time, which I thought was a good sign for my time problem. Waiting till morning makes sense to me, leaving at night would be rather obvious. Don't you think I asked? Somehow I must have convinced Jeff. He seemed to calm way down and Sandy turned on the T.V. We stayed in the rest of the night. It was one of the longest nights I can remember. Jeff was rather quiet all night and fell asleep early. Sandy and I talked quite a bit. She really was a very nice girl. She had just gotten herself into a bad relationship with Jeff, and would figure that out later. I was very nervous and anxious, not knowing what I was going to do about my suitcase, and how I would eventually have to make a break for it. One thing was for sure, I was never more ready to get as far away from Jeff and

Sandy as I could possibly get. Sandy got naked and jumped under the covers. What a magnificent sight. I never grew tired of seeing her body, that's for sure, it was flawless. I did the same and we both crashed.

In the morning, my rude awakening was Jeff hitting me in the face with the car keys. He was really mad. He ordered me to check out the stairs, the exits and go look around the lobby too. Bring me back some Black Mollies. I'm going to need them for the long drive, he ordered. I quickly dressed and was out the door in a flash. In the hallway by the steps leading down to the garage was a different security officer, nonetheless they were still covered. I walked over and pushed the elevator button to go down to the lobby. Nothing had changed, security was tight. I walked over to the phone booth to think again. Trying to come up with a plan, I noticed that if you weren't carrying luggage they didn't stop you. I took a chance and walked right out the front door. No one approached me or seemed suspicious of me. I thought about leaving my things in the room and getting away and not returning till 9:00a.m. I had the car keys. That wouldn't work. I had the notion to at least leave them the car keys. After walking around the outside of the hotel just looking around, everything looked normal and it seemed that it would be cool to approach the vehicle. I opened the trunk and Sandy's suitcase. It was full of gallon size zip lock bags stuffed with pills, uppers, downers, in different shapes and sizes, all different colors. I had never seen so many pills in all my life. I shut the suitcase and then the trunk really fast. I had to move quickly time was of the essence. On my way back through the lobby, to my surprise, I ran into Marion. She gave me a big hug and a kiss. We're leaving for home in about thirty minutes, she happily announced. This is goodbye, it was nice getting to know you and spending some quality time with you. I'll never forget you. You're such a southern gentleman. You too, you were so cool. Do you think I could write to you? Sure, let me get a pen and paper from the front desk, she replied. In that instance, it hit me. Maybe Marion would be willing to help me out of this jam. It certainly wouldn't hurt to try, seeing how they were going to check out and all. After hurriedly explaining my dilemma, she agreed to help me with my suitcase. My plan is to meet David out in front of the hotel at 9:00a.m. If there is any way you could meet me at the phone booth between 8:50-9:00a.m., I will pass you my suitcase and then if you would please meet me out front, that would be the only way, I explained. Marion agreed and said she would meet me in just a few minutes. It was perfect. I looked at my watch, 8:30a.m., I'd have to hurry. I only have thirty minutes to pull this off. Everything began to fall into place. Suddenly I had a really good game plan that was just crazy enough to work. It was going to be close, I was running out of time, but somehow, I pray this works, and I made the sign of the cross. I try to be Catholic, well I was raised, a Catholic. I felt pretty good about everything. It was as if someone was watching over me that morning. I hurried up to the room and handed Jeff the pills and the car keys. Sandy was in the shower, I could hear the water running. I lied to Jeff and told him the coast was clear by the staircase leading to the parking garage. Knowing that waiting for Sandy to finish her shower and getting dressed would buy me some time, I grabbed my suitcase. As I headed for the door Jeff said they'd meet me at the car in five minutes. I'll be waiting, hurry please, I said. The time to make our move is right now, come on, I said with convincing urgency and I split without looking back. When I got down to the lobby I could see that Marion was by the phone booth already waiting for me. Things seemed to be falling into place perfectly. I handed off the suitcase without a word being said. She fell in with the rest of her family like nothing was happening. I called room 707 and Ron answered and said David was getting the jeep and was going to meet me at 9:00. Good luck and nice to have met you, Ron said. Likewise, you are the greatest. I went straight out the front door of the hotel empty handed, never looking back. Seconds later, out comes Marion suitcase in hand. You couldn't have timed it any better as David pulled up in the jeep. I grabbed the suitcase, thanked Marion, kissed her goodbye and promised her I would write as soon as I got back to San Antonio. I jumped into the jeep and David made a quick getaway. The great escape had worked, I was free. As we headed for the highway I thanked God I was finally far away from Jeff and would never see him again. I made a promise to myself to learn to make better choices in the future and to know who you are dealing with before getting too involved. I made the sign of the cross and looked up to the heavens above. Thank you Jesus, I said out loud. David told me to relax, and that everything was going to be fine. Brother you're in good hands now, as he extended his hand to shake my hand in friendship. I don't know what I would have done without you, thank you so much.

Chapter 10

Road Trip "Home"

It was a long way to Mexico City, six to eight hours by car, I wasn't quite sure I really couldn't remember. Besides Jeff had been driving so fast how could one calculate time. It was a beautiful warm sunshiny day, typical weather for this part of the country. I'm hoping to do some shopping and sightseeing along the way, I hope you don't mind stopping, David said, as he drove. You're not really in a big hurry are you? David asked. Now that I'm a free man I feel so relaxed it would be my pleasure. I'm definitely not in a rush. You're the captain and I'm your copilot, sounds like a good time. Have you ever experienced off road vehicles like this jeep? Not exactly, I'm not really sure what you're talking about. Well this jeep is built for climbing hills, rocky roads and mountains. It's equipped with off road tires and four wheel drive. Would you like to buckle up and have some fun? You can trust me, I wouldn't do anything to jeopardize the jeep or us, promise you that. Where? I asked. Coming up to this next mountain side will start our adventure. David knew what he was doing. It was a lot of fun, scary at times, but fun. I didn't know what that large grill in front of the jeep was for, but now I do. It mows down large bushes and small trees and shrubs and literally creates your own path or trail. We stopped on the very top of one of the larger hills and got out of the jeep to enjoy the view. Let's share the moment with some gold, Acapulco gold, David said, as he lit a rather large joint. Grab us a beer out of the ice chest please, he added. This is nice. You are one of the kindest people I've ever met. I'll never forget all that you have done for me, or this spectacular view. We don't have mountains in my area, I said. Canada has many, David explained, but they are all so very different. That's why I have this jeep. What do you say let's go down and get back on the highway and find a great spot to eat, I'm famished. I'll second that. While having our lunch we exchanged addresses and phone numbers. I promised David I would mail him a money order or check as soon as possible. I'm going to pay for this lunch, the gas, and of course the bus ticket. I'm forever in your debt brother. Don't mention it, just send the money. I would have probably ended up in jail, if not for your help. David just laughed, I trust you will, send the money, that is. Forever indebted to you brother, trust me, doing me this huge favor is so cool. I'm old school brother, as far as I'm concerned I owe you for life, ten times over. We finished our meal and got back on my journey home. It was a beautiful drive. Some of the towns were very ancient and historical looking. We stopped and visited a huge Cathedral. I must go in and say some prayers, I explained. David followed. I knelt and prayed for a few minutes. I thought about everything that I'd just experienced and realized I needed to reorganize my priorities. Study real hard, and learn some new guitar riffs. Maybe take some lessons. Hopefully meet a nice girl, maybe I'll get married, and settle down and have some kids, like what dad wants. Anyway, I thought, I'm going to change. I said a few Hail Mary's and some Our Father's and we left. We made a couple of more stops along the way and finally reached the downtown area. I asked for directions to the bus station and we were on our way. David was as ready to get there as I was.

Once we reached the station, I was in luck. The next bus going my way to Piedras Negras, (Black Rocks) the border town across from Eagle Pass, Texas was in about forty-five minutes. I thanked David again after he paid for my ticket all the way to San Antonio and handed me a ten dollar bill for food. Appreciate it, you are the greatest. David sat with me as we waited for my bus and continued talking about music and my future. I've learned a good lesson on this trip. It's time to grow up amigo. We said our goodbyes, and I thanked him one last time. As I boarded the bus I looked back at David and waved, thinking to myself and smiling at him, how lucky I had been to know him.

Once I was on the bus and in my seat, I began to contemplate all that I had just been through. I really felt very different suddenly, free and on my own again, thanks to David, and Marion. I made the sign of the cross and closed my eyes and prayed again. I promised Jesus I would be a smarter person and try to listen more to my parents. I'm really going to change for the better. I knew the bus ride to the border was a long one, (8-10hrs.) so I tried to get some sleep. I dozed of immediately. Dreaming I was in the clouds just floating freely. It was heavenly, free and on my own. I was on top of the world. When I awoke and looked at my watch, time had passed quickly while I was sleeping and the dream I was having seemed very real. Meaning I was free from Jeff. I was on an airplane and it felt like I was flying through the air without the airplane. Some of the dream could be lyrics to a song, I was singing in the dream, I imagined. I pulled out the pen and paper and began to write. Inspired, the verses came.

"A Long Morning"

Sitting alone in a daze

The smoke clouds up my empty room

Nothing seems to pay

I've made another grave error

For my dreams have moved

From near to far again

Truth of it all, comes in many colorful images

But not like I expected

Being accepted and rejected

I'm used to the shame

I'll move about to find

It's all the same

You've got to make it

Or just plain remain

It'll all come to me with time.

The wait is part of the long road.

I'm not sure why, but usually the lines I write just flow through me without much thought. I was never really sure if they made sense or if they were interesting or any good. All I knew was that they were original thoughts, and I always saved them somewhere. Usually not even remembering them, but I always signed and dated everything and have most, some I just can't find. I'm still looking for lost writings. I guess I didn't think to always save them together in the same folder. I've found a few in several different guitar cases. Some of my short stories were in an old folder in my dresser drawer. Some verses scattered in my desk. Sometimes I can remember a piece and can't find it. That drives me crazy.

The bus made several stops on the long journey to the border. Very nice scenic views along the highway made the ride very interesting. It was the same highway we had traveled but that was during the night and too dark to enjoy. My stomach was growling and I knew I would need something to eat before reaching the border. I figured I'd spend five dollars on food in Mexico, and the other five was for the three hour bus ride in Texas. The next town was a ten minute break, the driver announced. Exiting the bus quickly I found a lady selling chopped streak street tacos smothered in onions and cilantro. They were greasy on small corn tortillas, (sort of mini tacos) but they were very clean and very delicious. She had cokes and the best hot sauce. I had two plates of six. Remember, they're not like in the states, these you order by the half dozen or a dozen, minimum six to an order. After boarding the bus, I quickly dozed off again.

I'm not sure how long I slept, maybe an hour, but I was awakened by music and very loud singing. Traditionally in Mexico it's very common for a musician, guitar player, to board a bus on the highway going one way, then getting off, crossing the highway and return on another bus going back to his original starting point, maybe his hometown. Along the way he earns some loose change to possibly feed his family. The gentleman was a very good guitar player and had a great voice. He was quite the entertainer. Some passengers were amused as I (me being a musician) and cooperated along with a few others and placed some coins in his sombrero between songs, others were annoyed and just wanted to sleep. After the musician got off, there were others. Some quickly came in and offered chips, peanuts and candy, followed by another with the drinks. They sold what they could at different stops and exited very quickly. One lady offered us homemade tamales, and another tacos, I thought it was great. Everyone bought stuff, even the driver. You would never see anything like that in the states. After passing several small towns we seemed to pick up speed and began to descend from the higher altitude of Mexico City. I'm not sure how high but my ears clogged and then finally popped just like on an airplane. Breathing seemed easier as I took some deep breaths. The air is definitely thinner in Mexico City due to its elevation. My head had cleared from the drugs and I was beginning to feel like my old self again. I'll never do acid again, I promised myself. I was very happy, things could have been much worse. I began to feel very drowsy again, and fell back asleep.

I awoke refreshed. I must have slept three or four hours. Finally some of landscape began to look familiar. Some of the beautiful mountains looked vaguely familiar. I then realized we were getting close to a big city I had visited many times but wasn't sure, so I asked the lady seated next to me. Monterrey, she said. Cool, I'd been here many times in the late sixties in my Volkswagen Beetle bug. That meant that we were approximately four hours from the border of Nuevo Laredo. Crossing the bridge into Laredo, Texas, and another four hours or so to San Antonio was very exciting news. Fast approaching Monterrey, I began reminiscing, the great trips with my high school buddies, so cool. We would hit the Red Zone (La Zona Rosa Plaza) downtown. That's where the best hotels were and they had the best clubs. No one ever asked for I.D's. so we could drink, that's why kids from the States always came to Mexico in the first place, you could party hardy. Monterrey had the only Pizza Hut I had ever seen in Mexico, which we loved to hang out at. The only other restaurant that we frequented was the famous "El Rey Del Cabrito". They served all kinds of Mexican food but specialized in cabrito (goat). The younger the goat the more tender and delicious it was. Cabrito is a very famous delicacy in Mexico, very popular amongst the locals. Monterrey and Saltillo, Mexico were famous for cabrito. I can't remember the name of it but there was this one bowling alley in Monterrey. It always reminded us of home and of course it was one of the things we always did when we were in town. When you're way down in Mexico bowling is as American as you can get, and that back home feel is right there in our hearts longing for America, American. My favorite drive was a winding road up a large mountain all the way to the top. Around and around, up, up and away, it was a long way up but well worth it. You had to be extra careful, I remembered because the two way road is very narrow and steep, there is no place to pull over and the only way is up or down. Any missed turn could mean falling off the side of the mountain, ouch, instant death. I guess that was partly what made it so challenging and exciting. "Chepinque Park" was at the top of the list of places to visit for me every time. I never failed to visit. Once you got to the top, the view was incredible. There was a motel with a pool and restaurant. You could rent small cabana (cabins) rooms on the side of the mountain. It was really neat. Gosh we had some good times there. The ten minute stop at the bus station was great. I'd been here many times when I was a kid traveling from Monclova to Monterrey. I usually would be in the family car and in my mother's home town of Monclova. It's a very small town, not much to do. As I got older, we began to take a bus trip, which was a two hour drive to Monterrey. Monterrey being a much bigger town had lots more to do. As I exited the bus the familiar smell of hot dogs was in the air. I entered the station and headed for the men's room. On the way back to the bus I couldn't resist the old man's cart and the picture of a great looking hot dog on the side of his rolling establishment. I counted my change and completed the buy. This will hold me till I get across the border and back in the good old U.S. of A. After my snack I managed to get some much needed sleep. Believe it or not I still felt some of the effects of the acid. As if ascending back to earth and reality quickly, but I felt great, free, back on my own. Thinking back over the last two weeks, I had felt helplessly trapped and controlled most of the time by Jeff. I'll never fall into that situation again I promised myself. The driver's intercom announcement woke me and we were told to gather our belongings, you will be transferring to a different bus, welcome to Nuevo Laredo. Most of the passengers had reached their destination. The rest of us boarded a van headed across the border into Laredo, Texas to our bus continuing the route into Texas. I was so happy my ticket was paid in full all the way to San Antonio. I was almost out of cash. It was a quick ride in the van with one stop at U.S. Customs at the border crossing. I was asked a single question. Are you an American citizen? Yes sir, I replied. That was it. They didn't even bother to open my suitcase. I was back in the van in a flash. It was quick and easy for all of us, what a relief, I had heard some horrific stories and wasn't quite sure what to expect. Reaching the van's final stop the Greyhound bus station in Laredo, Texas, we were told it would be an hour wait for our connecting bus. That didn't seem so bad, it could have been longer, I thought.

Boarding the bus for the final home stretch, I thought about my mom and dad and all four of my sisters, family, it's nice to have family. I truly had missed them all very much. I never did make that call. Fortunately I did send the postcards. The four hour ride was pretty much uneventful and quick, considering the long trip I had just endured. Along the way I tried to prioritize my life and goals. How things were going to be different from now on. I felt much more worldly, knowledgeable and mature. I think somehow I grew from this experience. I could see the Tower of America's, San Antonio's space needle and the Hemisfair Park ski line fast approaching, home sweet home. Pulling into the bus station and exiting the bus, I was so happy to be home, I could have kissed the ground.

Chapter Eleven

How Sweet It Is

"Home"

I was craving my mother's home cooking. As soon as I walked through the door I asked, what smells so good? She laughed and asked why I hadn't called? Food, aren't you going to say hello first. I gave mother a big hug and kissed her on the lips. I'm sorry, I apologize, never did make that call. We were worried about you son, you were supposed to call. You got all of my postcards, right? No, mother laughed, letters and postcards can take weeks to arrive in the States, silly. Something I didn't know. We haven't got a one. Great we can read them together, I said jokingly. How and where is dad? In his bedroom resting after a long day's work, something you should learn to do soon. Okay, okay I get it. I'm in school, plenty of time to get a job soon, I promised. Thinking back after things had gotten a little weird in Acapulco, I had decided not to call from the Holiday Inn. I was sure that if something went wrong they would find me via phone call listings. Call me a little paranoid. Not having much money it made sense not to call from anyplace else, economically speaking. I was only glad that early in the vacation I had bought some stamps and the postcards in the hotel lobby. It never came to mind when or how long they would take to arrive in San Antonio. In them I had mentioned to my dad to please feed my Doberman, Candy. I'd had her for many years. And had mentioned how things were going well for us. Acapulco is beautiful, as these postcards shows. It didn't take long to smooth things over with the folks, as usual. They were just glad I was home and that everything had gone so well for me.

Christmas break from school was over and I was just in time for my second semester at San Antonio College. After my very first day of school I was right back to my usual routine, the neighborhood pool hall, on my way home. I joined a few friends on one of the pool tables for a friendly game of Eight ball partners for a beer. After about an hour or so we decided to pay for our pool time at the register. The bartender comes over to me and asks where I had been and where my two friends were. Which ones I asked? The older fellow and the young beautiful blonde, you remember, about two weeks ago. Well anyway, he explains, the following day, after the last time you were in here, there were these two plain clothes detectives asking a lot of questions and they showed us some pictures of your friends. My knees began to shake I got so nervous. What's up, what did they say, I asked? Well it seems they're wanted in Florida in connection with some warrants and charges of armed robbery or burglary of a drug store, transporting a stolen vehicle across state lines, stolen property, fraud, identity theft, and kidnapping of a minor and taking her across state lines, just to mention the ones I can remember. At no time had I mentioned to anyone other than my family that I had gone to Acapulco with Sandy and Jeff. I played it off and pretended not to know anything about the situation and left. As I got behind the steering wheel of my car everything began to make sense. Their actions, step by step the pieces of the puzzle began to fall into place. I thought back, how I met Jeff. Then Sandy, the perfect persuader, how vulnerable, so naïve, so horny. The whole time I was being set up conned into going. They needed me to help them escape into Mexico, what a kid, what a fool. I could have gotten in a lot of trouble and still may. Jeff going into the bedroom at my girlfriend's apartment that first night, Sandy coming onto me, it was all planned out perfectly to convince me to go. How brilliant, ingenious, the plan was to get the Mexican kid's help. Jeff sending the goods via Greyhound, beautiful, smart, the evidence, the goods, would follow them here to San Antonio from Florida, how perfect. The package, the box loaded with pills from the drug store heist, guns, money, and marijuana, wow. And I the Mexican scapegoat, so stupid, so gullible, so naïve and trusting of people, I fell prey, perfect for their escape.

The months went by and everything was fine. Nothing had ever come up again about Acapulco, the trip, Sandy or Jeff. Till one afternoon, I was in my bedroom doing a little homework. My mother called out to me, phone call for you son. To my surprise it was Jeff. Hey, how are you? Ready for another adventure, he asked? Everything is cool, we got caught. What do you mean? I asked. Yea Sandy and I got caught in Acapulco trying to get out of the hotel. They had our pictures, they weren't looking for you, you're cool, I made sure of that, Jeff says. No hard feelings right? Yea, we did a little time in Acapulco, then got extradited to Florida, I'm sorry I'll try and explain. Let's see, my family, well mom, sent the entire amount owed for fines and the Holiday Inn stay, tax and title. Then the authorities from Florida took over and took us back to face the music, guilty as charged. My family got us a good lawyer, the best money can buy. I took the entire rap. Sandy played the victim and got off completely. She talked her family into dropping the kidnapping charges and my mother gave them a settlement check. Mom made me apologize to my older brother for stealing his car and his Gold American Express card. She paid the entire balance plus whatever he owed from before, and he was happy. And of course I had to promise him I wouldn't do it again. Your name was never even mentioned. My lawyers just kept postponing and postponing the trial and somehow got me off on some sort of technicality. They probably paid someone off with some of the money my mother gave them. So how have you been? What do you say, want to do some driving? I'm doing just fine, back at college. Yea, Sandy's in school too, we're waiting for the semester to end and we'll be coming your way and onto Los Angeles, California. What do you think? Interested, I'll pay you to help with the driving and all your expenses too. Well, I said, almost speechless from disbelief, I've met a nice girl and we're really tight. I've also got a part time job and during the upcoming summer they want me to work full time, imagine that, good pay too. So thanks for the invite but I think I'm going to have to pass Jeff, say hi to Sandy for me, maybe next time, my mom is calling me I've got to go, bye, Jeff, have a good trip. I never saw or heard from Jeff or Sandy again, that was forty four years ago.

The End

Copy Right: 2014
The Doctor
Alfred De La Zerda

All Rights Reserved
ISBN-13:978-1495456138
ISBN-10:1495456137

To order additional copies of this book go to amazon.com or createspace.com

243

Made in the USA
San Bernardino, CA
13 May 2014